PPRAISE FOF

MW01528324

"*Justice Restored* is a much needed roadmap back to the constitutional system of justice intended for *all*. This book is a must read for every politician to remind [us] of our true purpose in government and as a guide on how to bring our nation to equal justice for all, rather than just the few who can afford it."

—Vera Reynolds, state congressional candidate and
NAACP chapter chairman, North Carolina

"*Justice Restored* is a must read of our time! I have observed a lot of injustice in this country. Howell Woltz speaks exactly to the truth and challenges we are facing in our justice system as citizens of what is considered to be the 'best country in the free world.'"

—Lamont Banks, executive director, A Just Cause

"Howell Woltz understands the shortcomings of the American system of justice—and what to do about it—better than anyone I know. He has lived it and knows the truth of our failed system—and how to restore it back to life. This should be required reading for every lawyer, judge, prosecutor, citizen, and student of criminal justice."

—Charlie Engle, ultrarunner, criminal justice survivor,
and author of *Running Man*

"In *Justice Restored* Howell shows us the redemptive promise of the rule of law when fairly applied as well as our collective responsibility to protect it so that it can protect us."

—Mike Pace and Tim Isaacs,
Center for Teaching the Rule of Law

"Howell's intellect, passion, and incredible experience have put him in the unique position to tell us what's really wrong and how to right it in the American system of justice. Enough innocent Americans have been targeted and illegally prosecuted. *Justice Restored* is the roadmap back to due process of law."

—Lewis Borsellino, author *The Day Trader*

Justice Restored

10 STEPS TO END MASS INCARCERATION IN AMERICA

Howell W. Woltz

HybridGlobal
PUBLISHING

Published by
Hybrid Global Publishing
355 Lexington Press
New York, NY 10017

Manufactured in the United States of America, or in the United Kingdom when distributed elsewhere.

Author: Woltz, Howell W.
  Title: Justice Restored: Ten Steps to End Mass Incarceration in America
  ISBN:
  Hardcover: 9781938015496
  Paperback: 9781938015472
  eBook: 9781938015489

Cover design by: Joe Potter and David Deasy
Cover photo: National Archives and Records Administration.
Interior design: Scribe Inc

Author's URL: www.howellwoltz.com

DEDICATION

To my brother Jim Woltz and his wife, Jill—a better support group has never been found.

I would also like to thank the hundreds of sufferers met along the way who shared their stories (and files) proving that the injustices done them were not one-off events, but indisputable evidence of systemic corruption and denial of due process of law by the courts of the United States of America.

The national disgrace of mass incarceration must be remedied. That can be accomplished by simply restoring due process of law, and I further dedicate this book to those brave souls working to that end, often putting themselves in danger in the process.

Howell Woltz [in tie] is surrounded by students seeking information after giving his talk on eroding freedoms at Mount Airy High School [TIMES Photo—Maloy]

Woltz Fears Loss Of Freedoms

"I want to frighten you, excite you and encourage you to act to hold on to your fleeting freedoms so you won't have to spend your later years in submission."

This said, Howell Woltz went on to explain to students assembled in the auditorium three dollars in administrative costs to give away the same amount, Woltz said, "Instead of more bureaucracy, we need more churches."

Accusing the federal government of using tax dollars in virtual from the

In ending Woltz said, "The worst and scariest thing about this is that every word I've said is true.

Following his talk Woltz passed out literature for Young Americans for Freedom, and took names of

CONTENTS

ACKNOWLEDGMENTS

My thanks to Laura Pitter, attorney with Human Rights Watch in New York City, as well as former federal judge, Art Strickland (Virginia) and Attorney Randy James (North Carolina) for their advice, unending assistance and for being my sounding board(s).

To my deceased grandfather, Attorney, H.O. Woltz, Sr., I owe a special debt of gratitude for countless hours in my younger years, teaching me what the law was supposed to be (and do) in this nation, and for allowing me to witness the process first-hand in the courts. Without this direct experience of seeing Constitutional courts in operation as a young man, I might not have had a reference point to see how badly the legislatures at both the national and state levels have eroded our Constitutional rights over the past half-century.

I also wish to thank my literary agent, Janet Goldstein, for making this book commercially viable and for her friendship.

PREFACE

On September 15, 1977, our local newspaper, *The Mount Airy Times*, ran a story about a speech I had just delivered exploring what I saw, at the time, as a frightening trend in America: the dramatic increase in government control over our lives. I warned the audience that the trends we were beginning to see—in 1977—had caused the downfall of "twenty-three democracies, usually in less than two-hundred years, throughout [human] history." I worried that the United States would soon follow that trend, as the headline of the article, "Woltz Fears Loss of Freedoms," indicated. Today, nearly 40 years later, it's clear those fears have not only come true, they have exceeded my wildest nightmares.

Fast-forward to 2016. I no longer call the United States of America home. I live in a former Soviet Bloc nation in Central Europe—the kind of place I grew up believing was less free than the great nation of my birth. And, ironically, I live with more freedom as an expatriate in a strange land than I could ever hope to experience in my own country.

Almost every day, the headlines from the Land of the Free prove me correct. Today, as I complete this book in Central Europe, CNN journalist Jeremy Diamond is reporting that the U.S. has fallen 29 more places—to rank a dismal 49th in the world—in Freedom of the Press. This unprecedented, 29-point drop on President Barack Obama's watch follows an already embarrassing plummet to 20th place that took place during President George W. Bush's administration. We now rank behind many of our former enemies—something that is probably unimaginable to most Americans.[1] And this trend away from freedom in the United States seems to gain momentum regardless of which political party is at the helm.

In fact, the Obama administration has imprisoned more journalists and whistleblowers, according to the watchdog group Reporters Without Borders, than at any time before in our history. Obama broke the record held by that of his predecessor in the White House, President Bush, who presided over a period in our history that is of particular significance to me. Because in 2006, after 30 years spent exposing government wrongdoing, I became one of the 55 journalists and whistleblowers imprisoned by the Bush administration.

After that speech back in 1977, I became a columnist, and continued until I realized I had to get a "real job" and make a living. However, I continued writing and giving public talks about the State of our Union, warning—like the mythical Cassandra[2]—about the erosion of our constitutional rights and freedoms. I continued this work up until 2015, when I had to leave the United States to keep from being jailed again by the even more zealous Obama Administration. I had already learned the hard way that dissent in America is no longer tolerated.[3]

It's almost impossible to read the news today without being horrified by the scope of this problem. A Columbia Law School study, recently disclosed in *The New Yorker* magazine, revealed that, in an intensive review by courts of almost every capital case over a 26-year period (at both state and federal level), our

---

1 http://edition.cnn.com/2015/02/13/politics/u-s-press-freedom-ranking
   -obama-administration-leaks/.
2 Cassandra was the daughter of the last King of Troy, in Greek mythology, who was said to have the gift of prophecy, but when she refused to sleep with Apollo, she was cursed by the god, that though her words were always true—no one would believe them.
3 I was also illegally taken and held by the U.S. government in 2006, though never convicted in or by any court of jurisdiction for any crime.

courts had a proven error rate of 73 percent—yes—73 *per-cent*. Nearly three out of four death penalty convictions, the study proved, were in error. The courts of America had either convicted an innocent person, or so violated his or her rights as to make the outcome undependable, requiring overturn.

In addition to those thousands who were wrongfully put to death or sent to death row, the erosion of the rights of due process of law, combined with the virtual elimination of *habeas corpus* (our right to challenge wrongful imprisonment) in 1996, has put millions more wrongfully behind bars.

I personally knew this to be true, not only from the 87 months I spent in prison, but from the work I did on over 400 non-capital cases (where the error rate is actually higher, in my experience) since 2006. I dedicated my years in the American gulag to working on hundreds of cases in addition to my own, and learned from inside the system just how widespread our mass incarceration problem has become. However, seeing it acknowledged in black and white, by one of the world's most prestigious law schools, made it somehow more real. There was proof that the majority of the executions performed in this country before the study concluded in 1996 were little more than state-sanctioned murders, and the imprisonments were little more than state crimes.

Just how many people could have been victimized? The study included cases from 1973 through 1996—the year when Americans' constitutional right to challenge such errors was taken. I remembered seeing some sort of admission by the Department of Justice as to just how many Americans were included in this group, and began digging through the mountains of statistics I'd collected over the years of writing about this problem.

I finally found the article I was looking for in the early morning hours here in Central Europe—just about the time America was going to bed. It was in a small box of papers I brought with me when I left the States, which included an article from the U.S. Department of Justice's *BNA Criminal Law Reporter*

(May 19th, 2010, issue; Vol. 87, No.7). That article stated, "The U.S. Department of Justice estimates that 71 million people—approximately 25 percent of the American population—have a criminal record."

I had saved the article for two reasons. First, because that was the only time I had ever seen an actual admission from our government of exactly how many Americans had been assigned the label of felon. The second was that the government admitted that this label applied to 25 percent of the entire nation—a percentage which, in any other country, would have been cause for revolution.

Back in the spring of 2010, 71 million adults—one of every four Americans over 18—already had a criminal record.

My mind whirled. These numbers were inconceivable, and beyond anything, to my knowledge, that had ever occurred in human history. One out of every four American citizens had been labeled or made into a "criminal" by their government, and now that same government had admitted that three out of every four of them had been wrongfully convicted. That was millions and millions of American citizens, violated in such a heinous fashion, by the nation that presents itself to the world as the leader in freedom and justice. At that moment, I decided the myth needed to be exploded.

I researched the statistics on every brutal dictator and thug I could remember by name or nation, but none came close to the number of citizens imprisoned by Ronald W. Reagan, George H.W. Bush, William J. Clinton, George W. Bush, and Barack H. Obama. Then I took the Department of Justice's estimate of the number of convicted citizens from 2010—71 million—and applied the 73 percent error rate proven by the Columbia Law School study.

The number I came up with? 51,830,000. That's the number, America. Almost 52 million of your friends, your family members, your fellow citizens have been wrongfully imprisoned and/or murdered by United States prosecutors and courts since 1973.

I could not breathe for a moment. Seeing this number in black and white—confirmed by the same governments and courts that had propagated these crimes—was almost too much to absorb. But the only other possibility was that those same courts and U.S. government entities were misrepresenting the evil they themselves have done. That seemed highly unlikely.

But how could my beloved country—the freest nation on earth, as recently as my childhood—have wrongfully imprisoned and executed 52 million of its own citizens, just since I was a student in college?

I sent my sources and calculations to friends at Human Rights Watch in New York and other human rights advocates around the world, justice reform advocates on both sides of the political divide, the United Nations, Council of Europe, as well as federal judges and attorneys across the United States. I begged any of them to prove me wrong. I also announced my findings on the U.S. radio show *A Just Cause*.[4]

Soon afterward, a copy of the article about me that appeared back in 1977 appeared in my email inbox, along with a warning to be quiet. Who sent the email? The sender's address had been blocked, but for some reason, this particular email did not wind up in my spam folder. *The Mount Airy Times* went out of business 25 years ago, and not many people would have access to the archives. Clearly, whoever sent that email has some degree of power. However, he or she is not going to stop me.

Things need to change—and this is the roadmap.

Howell W. Woltz
July 2016

---

4 http://www.blogtalkradio.com/ajcradio2/2016/03/23/a-just-cause--the-fear
   -factor-government-intimidation-in-america.

INTRODUCTION

Once rarely discussed in America, the topic of mass incarceration has emerged as one of the most important social issues of the day. Both sides of the political aisle and national debate are currently clamoring to claim this space as their own—which is ironic, since both sides share more or less equal blame for creating this disaster in the first place.

From Republican "Get Tough on Crime" initiatives like Nixon's War on Drugs and Reagan's "conspiracy statutes" to Clinton and the Democrats' misguided attempt to outdo the Republicans with the Omnibus Crime Bill of 1994 and the refusal of the Bush or Obama administrations to seriously address the problems created by these actions, American taxpayers and due process of law have been the losers. The United States now has the largest prison population in human history, bar none. No dictator or tyrant on earth has ever come close to what our political leaders have done to the citizens of the United States in terms of imprisoning them *en masse*.

So why are both parties now vying to be seen as the one to successfully undo the system they created? Perhaps because, according to the U.S. Department of Justice, one in four Americans now has a criminal record. Many (if not most) of these citizens have suffered the injustice of being denied due process of law. Now, 71 million-plus Americans who have been branded with the Scarlet "F" (for felon) for the rest of their lives have become a permanent underclass, as have many of their families. It's a national disgrace, and a very public one, because almost every American now knows a victim—or has been one themselves.

In short, the mass incarceration machine has been working too well. And the people who are finally revealing how broken and distorted our system of justice has become are not from the media, as one might hope. Instead, the stories are coming from people who have experienced it firsthand, or watched a loved one destroyed by its grasp.

The news is also spreading internationally, further reducing (if not eliminating entirely) any moral authority the United States might have once claimed among other nations. The "Land of the Free" has not-so-jokingly become known as "The Incarceration Nation."

The United States has also come under serious international criticism for taking the rights of citizenship from the millions of people it convicts—for years or for life—leaving them without a voice in their own government. People cannot vote once they've been assigned the Scarlet "F." This has effectively rendered one-quarter of America of no interest to the lawmakers when running for election, completely disenfranchising them at the hands of the political class.

I recently met with a congressional leader who voiced this attitude. When I initially approached him during the summer of 2015 and asked for an appointment to discuss mass incarceration, his response was, "Why should I care about them (felons)? They can't vote." I reminded him that prior to 1964, African Americans had been similarly disenfranchised by Congress, and had loyally followed "the party of Lincoln" up until the Democratic Party re-enfranchised them through the Voting Rights Act. Overnight, the vast majority of African Americans left the Republican Party, became Democrats for life, and for generations to follow.

Unfortunately, victims of the American system of justice lose more than just their right to vote—they also lose their right to defend themselves (and their families), and they must pay taxes while being blocked from accessing many of the programs and services their tax dollars pay for. It's ironic that "Taxation Without Representation," which was the rallying cry for The American Revolution in 1776, has now been codified and systemized by the United States Congress, effectively preventing an underclass from challenging those who have deprived them of their voice. Even worse, this quarter of our nation's population are also not likely to find good, stable jobs, and will be shunned by many in our society forever.

I suggest that this aberration has already done permanent damage to our nation as a whole. Historically, governments that have disenfranchised a large proportion of their people or forced them into a permanent underclass without access or voice have faced unpleasant outcomes.

I must also point out that if the majority of the 71 million-plus Americans who have been incarcerated were actually guilty of crimes like murder, rape, robbery, arson, or aggravated assault, I would not waste my time working for their re-enfranchisement. Dangerous people need to be kept away from society until they can be rehabilitated. But I'm not talking about criminals who have been charged, fairly tried, and found guilty. I'm talking about people who have been falsely imprisoned and forced to plead guilty based on fabricated evidence or threats from prosecutors. I'm talking about the 47 percent who are nonviolent offenders still being arrested or kept in prison for smoking marijuana (when it is now legal in many states). I am talking about people who have harmed no one but themselves, but are in prison as if they had hurt someone else. These groups collectively account for 95 percent of our nation's prisoners today. And as some states have begun letting some of these prisoners go, a funny thing has happened. Crime rates have gone *down* in each state where mass releases have taken place over the past five years—proving these people were never a danger to society in the first place.

So why were so many of them in prison? Possibly because, over recent decades, Congress has passed (outside of its authority) some 314,000 new laws that can imprison free people and take their rights. This list does not even take into account the myriad of statutes concocted by state legislatures to fill their prisons. And while I'm certainly not suggesting that all of our laws are illegitimate, even the most sycophantic lover of government must admit that outlawing more than 314,000 human behaviors that were not considered wrong or criminal for most of human history is a bit excessive.

Have you collected rainwater from your own roof? Have you helped a mammal escape from a fishing net? Have you mistreated a mailbag? Have you simply thought about committing a crime or made an offhand comment to a colleague that might be interpreted as suggesting that a law *might* be broken in the future? If the answer to any of these (or 300,000-plus other) questions is in the affirmative, then *you are a criminal,* and that last crime—the crime of conspiracy—could put you in prison for longer than if you had actually done something.

In fact, 90 percent of federal cases today include a charge of some "conspiracy" to commit a crime. This simple inclusion makes a case a sure win for the prosecutor, because there is no real defense against a charge of *thinking* about breaking a law. If just two people who you may or may not know say that you thought about or considered breaking any of these thousands of laws, that's all the evidence the government needs to find you guilty. And many of these "tellers" don't tell the truth, as they are often offered leniency or avoidance of prosecution in exchange for testimony that will make the government's case against you.

As a patriotic American whose passion has been the study of our founding, our founders, and the amazing system of due process of law they established, I find this very troubling. I'm sure our founders believed The Bill of Rights would stand for all time, and never expected our own elected representatives would be the ones to rob us of them. However, I have seen the First (freedom of religion and press), Fourth (freedom from unreasonable search and seizure), Fifth (freedom from prosecution without due process of law), Sixth (the right to a speedy trial by an impartial jury), and Eighth Amendments (freedom from excessive bail, fines, and cruel and unusual punishment) of the Bill of Rights all but disappear in my lifetime. And after seven years of working on over 400 criminal cases, I must now reluctantly conclude that the United States judicial system is no longer about finding the truth. What's called "justice" is about getting another "win" for the prosecutor and filling our prisons to overflowing to feed America's fastest growing business—the prison industrial complex. Justice went out the window with Perry Mason.

The good news is, we as a people have the power to change this. What I propose is that we move beyond labels of "right and left" and focus on *right* and *wrong*. What we are now doing is wrong, and it must stop. We must move back to a system designed to produce a just outcome rather than an expeditious one where the government always wins.

This book presents 10 basic steps that, if taken, will restore our nation to the Rule of Law that will give everyone a fair chance in our legal system. Each chapter presents a real-life case study illustrating a problem, describes the issue's history, and proposes a precise solution. These solutions are simple, straightforward, and almost exclusively revolve around principles that have been abandoned by our courts and legislatures over the past thirty years. They are drawn from my intensive study of and participation in over 400 criminal cases, along with 40 years studying the documents, history, debates, and legal foundations which were intended to prevent this erosion of rights from ever happening in the United States of America.

We can do better. We must do better. And fortunately, it is as simple as demanding our leaders restore just three overriding principles that existed for most of our nation's history:

1. No one is above the law nor has immunity from punishment for its violation, regardless of position, status, wealth, or office.
2. A denial of due process of law should nullify a negative outcome; i.e., if a person is found to have been imprisoned based on errors or abuse of due process, his or her conviction must be voided.
3. Any statute, rule, or order which violates constitutional protections can have no force of law and, if applied, is cause for nullification of a conviction as well.

Justice Restored is the roadmap. Ten steps back to Rule of Law, back to due process, back to our basic principles of fairness and equity where justice is served rather than put into service. If followed and applied, these 10 steps will quickly put an end to the human tragedy of mass incarceration in the United States of America.

CHAPTER 1

Restore Habeas Corpus

Habeas Corpus is Latin for "you have the body." It is also a constitutional right (Section 9, Article 1, U.S. Constitution) for anyone who is imprisoned or whose liberty is restrained to demand to be brought before a court of jurisdiction where his or her captors must explain the cause of that restraint.

At least it *was* a sacred right from 1776 until 1996. While it remains part of the U.S. Constitution, in 1996 Congress gutted our right of *habeas corpus* and then-President Bill Clinton signed its death warrant with the passage of the Anti-Terrorism Effective Death Penalty Act (A.E.D.P.A.). This act was wholeheartedly supported by both Republicans and Democrats alike, so I'm not just blaming President Clinton for this contribution to our prison-industrial complex, any more than I would blame President Reagan for the passage of the conspiracy laws of the previous decade. As you will see throughout this book, both sides of the political divide are guilty.

The guardian of liberty for centuries, *habeas corpus* is not new, nor is it American in origin. The first recorded writ of *habeas corpus* was delivered to a court in England in 1305, while the writ's actual use precedes even the Magna Carta, which was signed between English nobles and King John in the year 1215. Over the centuries that followed, this tool of justice was used to free thousands of individuals—women improperly imprisoned in their homes by their husbands, so-called "heretics" illegally held by the Church, and even prisoners held by kings who failed to follow due process of law—earning it the moniker "The Great Writ of Liberty." Today, the loss of this powerful right may well be the harbinger of liberty's ultimate loss.

In his June 21, 2015, piece entitled "The Destruction of Defendants' Rights," Leonard Caplan of *The New Yorker* wrote, "The Anti-Terrorism and Effective Death Penalty Act of 1996 (A.E.D.P.A.) is surely one of the worst statutes ever passed by Congress and signed into law by a President. The heart of the law is a provision saying that, even when a state court misapplies the Constitution, a defendant cannot necessarily have his day in federal court. Instead, he must prove that the state court's decision was 'contrary to' what the Supreme Court has determined is 'clearly established federal law,' or that the decision was 'an unreasonable application of' it."

What this means in simple terms is that no matter how badly a state court violates the constitutional rights of its citizens, those citizens cannot use their right of *habeas corpus* to seek relief in the federal courts until years later, when (or if) they have exhausted every court in their state—a process that few can afford or survive.

Since A.E.D.P.A. gutted the right of *habeas corpus* at the federal level in 1996, there has been an explosion of unlawful convictions at both the state and federal level. And with the A.E.D.P.A. in place, those convicted have little if any means of ever correcting those injustices. This is a decimation of all of our rights as Americans—the only real winner is the burgeoning prison industry.

Mr. Caplan's article goes on to say, "A landmark Columbia Law School study of virtually every state and federal death-penalty appeal from 1973 to 1995 reported that the 'courts found serious, reversible error in nearly 7 of every 10 of the thousands of capital sentences that were fully reviewed during the period.' There were so many mistakes, the study found, that after 'state courts threw out 47% of death sentences due to serious flaws, a later federal review found "serious error"—error undermining the reliability of the outcome—in 40% of the remaining sentences.' " Without federal *habeas corpus*, those serious errors would have gone unchecked. Instead of later being found not to deserve the death penalty, as happened in 73 percent of the cases, or instead of being found innocent, as happened in 9 percent of the cases, these defendants likely would have been put to death.

Seventy-three percent of the time, our state and federal courts have been proven to get it wrong, even when they are about to kill someone.

This raises a very serious question about the rest of our judicial system. How closely do our courts follow the law and Constitution in the millions of cases where someone's life is *not* in the balance? After almost a decade spent working on non-death penalty cases, I can tell you the answer: "Not very closely at all." I have yet to review a single case where the government and/or the court itself did not violate federal law and the U.S. Constitution in its process of conviction. Meaning, at least in my own experience, this institutionalized ineptitude (or indifference) is even worse in non-death penalty cases.

It's also important to remember that this 73 percent error rate in both state and federal death penalty cases is based on data from before 1996, when the A.E.D.P.A. effectively eliminated our previously inalienable right to challenge wrongful court decisions.

If you were a surgeon, mechanic, electrician, carpenter, manufacturer, or pretty much anything besides a United States judge or prosecutor, could you get away with a 73 percent error rate? Could three out of every four products you made turn out to be defective? Of course not. Your customers and the communities you served would run you out of town rather than allow you to continue to churn out defective products or deliver defective services, and then refuse to fix their errors.

But this is basically what Congress did when it created the A.E.D.P.A. The Act was billed as a money-saving measure to prevent lengthy appeals by those sentenced to death. In reality, it has acted as little more than a safeguard to keep government from having to take responsibility for its mistakes, rather than fix their (frequent) errors or expose them to the public. Today, prosecutors and judges know that victims of wrongful prosecution no longer have any real means to be heard, and they appear to be acting accordingly. With little if any chance of being challenged—ever—due process of law seems to have been forgotten by the courts, and the old adage "Better to let 10 guilty men go free, than improperly imprison one," has become, "Better to put 10 innocents to death, than be publicly exposed for getting one wrong."

Of course, the loss of *habeas corpus* effects more than just prisoners who are facing the death penalty. Since the passage of A.E.D.P.A. in 1996, illegal restraint by government has become epidemic, as there is no real means left to challenge it. Though federal law 18 U.S.C. § 3164(d) of the Federal Criminal Code requires both federal and state governments to release any prisoner detained for more than 90 days without trial, this law is simply no longer followed. Instead, prisoners in many cases are held without trial for years, or until they agree to "voluntarily" plead guilty, whether they are or not.

Would this happen if the law were followed and these prisoners were free to prepare for trial or challenge their illegal incarceration? Probably not. Instead, because there is no meaningful way to challenge them, and because they have been immune from prosecution for such violations of law since 1967, today's prosecutors and courts can and do hold citizens unlawfully until they can be coerced into pleading guilty. So the gutting of *habeas corpus* has directly led to hundreds of thousands of innocents filling our prisons.[1]

The roots of *habeas corpus* are found in the 39th clause of the Magna Carta, which reads "No man shall be arrested or imprisoned . . . except by the lawful judgment of his peers or by the law of the land." That same guarantee is in our own Constitution. Therefore, neither the U.S. Congress nor any president of the United States, past or present, should be able to rob of us this right, except during time of war. Simply taking the Oath of Office and promising to uphold the Constitution should automatically require our elected officials to restore this fundamental right to We the People.

But that is not our reality. And if that reality is going to change, the restoration of *habeas corpus* must be made a political issue for both parties. The next president, whomever he or she might be, must see to it that this sacred right is available once again. Because at a time when our courts and prosecutors are randomly targeting citizens and imprisoning them, when there is no real oversight, and when our right to challenge government's errors has been restricted beyond meaningful utility, we have never needed *habeas corpus* more.

Perhaps the most definitive book on this subject, *Habeas Corpus: From England to Empire*, by Paul D. Halliday (Belknap Press, 2010), provides the best gauge of how important this writ has been in Anglo-American *juris prudence* history. In Halliday's study of thousands of *habeas corpus* petitions covering a period of five hundred years, he writes, "Throughout

---

1 I was unlawfully arrested in 2006 and illegally held for 87 months by the United States government, though never tried or convicted by any court of jurisdiction. Due to this "gutting" of *habeas corpus* to which Mr. Caplan refers in his article, it took me 10 years, 10 court petitions, and a federal judge to undo the court and government crimes against me, so I speak from experience.

its history the central purpose of habeas corpus has been to provide the means by which the judge might find the place at which liberty and physical security could be protected simultaneously by ensuring that subjects were imprisoned only according to law."

During the decades leading up to the American Revolution, the King's Bench in England granted petitions for writs of *habeas corpus* and released those being illegally held at the incredible rate of 83 percent. From my own experiences with our judicial system, I suspect that the rate of those illegally held in U.S. jails and prisons today is even higher than in the time of King George—a leader we called a tyrant and waged war against. What might that king (or President George Washington, for that matter) say about the U.S. leaders who eliminated this right for which our founders fought and died?

In our post-A.E.D.P.A. era, U.S. courts currently grant petitions for a writ of *habeas corpus* at a rate nearing zero. We're living under a system of tyranny without even knowing it. And if you expect the Supreme Court to come to the aid of We the People, I suggest that is highly unlikely.[2] Since 1937, the high court has followed a policy of not challenging unconstitutional legislation if it was passed by the United States Congress, no matter how egregiously it violates what is still the ultimate law of the land.

So despite the fact that the Constitution is clear in stating, "The Privilege of the Writ of Habeas Corpus *shall not be*

---

2 "The switch in time that saved nine" is the name given to what was perceived as the sudden jurisprudential shift by Associate Justice Owen Roberts of the U.S. Supreme Court in West Coast Hotel Co. v. Parrish, 300 U.S. 379 (1937) after President Franklin D. Roosevelt threatened to add four of his own judges to the court (13 total) to eliminate the existing court's power to challenge his legislation as unconstitutional. The court's policy since then has been to not challenge any law passed by Congress, regardless of how unconstitutional it may be. As former House Judiciary Committee Chairman, James Clyburn, observed in 2008, "Almost nothing Congress does today can find root in the U.S. Constitution."

suspended, unless when in Cases of Rebellion or Invasion the public Safety may require it," that suspension has now become a *fait accompli*. A.E.D.P.A. is a *de facto* suspension of this right.

Contrast this with the situation back in 1861, when President Abraham Lincoln suspended *habeas corpus* to prevent the release of John Merryman, a state legislator from Maryland and Lincoln enemy, who had been arrested by Union troops. Chief Justice of the Supreme Court Roger Taney issued a ruling that President Lincoln did not have the authority to suspend The Great Writ, only Congress could do so. While President Lincoln ignored the Court's ruling (setting another dangerous precedent), *habeas corpus* was restored shortly after Lincoln's death by President Andrew Johnson, in Proclamation 148, signed December 1, 1865.

In 1948, Congress again restricted The Great Writ by substituting a watered-down version, 28 U.S.C. § 2255, which required the petitioner to file his or her motion for relief from wrongful imprisonment with the court where the error was made, as opposed to an independent court in the area where the prisoner was being held, which had been the practice for almost 1,000 years of Anglo-American judicial history. The reasoning, weak as it was, included the argument that courts in areas where prisons were located might be inundated by such petitions. However, the real reason, as stated in the Notes section of the Federal Code and Rules, was to restrict the number of filings. The new law certainly accomplished that goal.

Things got even worse a year later with the *Carvell v. United States* decision, 173 F.2d 348 (4th Cir. 1949) (per curiam), which judicially mandated that the same judge who made the alleged error was to hear the prisoner's motion for relief. Since judges (both in my experience and in the review of hundreds of such filings) rarely admit their own error(s), this change made the substitute petition more or less worthless. However, once the Fourth Circuit made this ruling, every other Circuit immediately adopted the decision. Only one (the First Circuit) has since recanted it as unfair, and now requires an independent judge to hear such petitions.[3]

Rule 4, Chapter 153 of the Federal Code, in the Notes regarding the history of this practice, admits that this is true, yet the practice remains, as does what is left of the substitute writ for *habeas corpus* relief—which, in reality, is a suspension of the writ rather than a substitute for it.

This brings us to 1996, during the bipartisan "get tough on crime" era, when the A.E.D.P.A. further shackled the Great Writ by limiting the time frame for a wrongfully imprisoned person to challenge the court's error to one year after his or her conviction. In reality, this one-year time frame frequently expires before the wrongfully convicted citizen even gets to prison or can obtain the copies of the case files needed to make a meaningful appeal, not to mention learn the law and procedure necessary to file such a motion.

So, how have the restrictions to *habeas corpus* of the 20th Century affected our prison population? Statistics for the period following the 1948 restriction are not available; however, they are for the post-A.E.D.P.A. period. According to the U.S. Department of Justice's Bureau of Justice Statistics, in 1995, the year before the A.E.D.P.A. was passed, the Bureau recorded 41,679 *habeas corpus* petitions. By the year 2000, that number had dropped to 25,504. The rate at which federal and state prison inmates filed civil rights petitions decreased from 37 to 19 per 1,000 inmates[4] during that same period of time.[5]

---

3   The Court of Appeals for the First Circuit has held that a judge other than the trial judge should rule on the 2255 motion. See Halliday v. United States, 380 F.2d 270 (1st Cir. 1967). Notes–Rule 4, Chapter 153.

4   Bureau of Justice Statistics, U.S. Department of Justice Special Report NCJ 189430, published January, 2002.

5   Commentators have been critical of having the motion decided by the trial judge. See Developments in the Law—Federal Habeas Corpus, 83 Harv.L.Rev. 1038, 1206–1208 (1970).

  '[T]he trial judge may have become so involved with the decision that it will be difficult for him to review it objectively. Nothing in the legislative

This is not a small percentage limited to special situations. Errors, weak legal representation, malpractice, and judicial and prosecutorial misconduct have led to millions of lives being unnecessarily ruined, leaving the victims with no reasonable means for seeking or obtaining relief.

The human cost of a system of justice where three of every four prisoners held behind bars should not be there is staggering. When a breadwinner/taxpayer/community member is falsely or wrongfully incarcerated, not only do they suffer, their families and communities suffer as well. Families frequently break apart due to the separation, even in cases where a marriage is only pending.[6] The community loses a productive member. And the wrongfully convicted citizen goes almost overnight from being a contributor to society to a drain on its resources. His or her life is, effectively, destroyed.

Clearly something about this process is very, very wrong.

The solution begins with the elimination of 28 U.S.C. § 2254 (state cases) and § 2255 (federal cases) and the restoration of our constitutional right to challenge court error. These substitute means of challenge, that were admittedly designed to restrict this right, clearly have only hindered justice rather than serve it.

Of equal if not greater importance, however, is the repeal of the A.E.D.P.A. As Mr. Caplan wrote, "The Anti-Terrorism

---

history suggests that "court" refers to a specific judge, and the procedural advantages of section 2255 are available whether or not the trial judge presides at the hearing.

The theory that Congress intended the trial judge to preside at a section 2255 hearing apparently originated in *Carvell v. United States*, 173 F.2d 348 (4th Cir. 1949) (per curiam), where the panel of judges included Chief Judge Parker of the Fourth Circuit, chairman of the Judicial Conference committee which drafted section 2255. But the legislative history does not indicate that Congress wanted the trial judge to preside.'

6 According to prison marriage expert Sheri Stritof in "Can a Marriage Survive a Prison Sentence?" the marriages of approximately 80 percent of men and almost 100 percent of incarcerated women end in divorce. Approximately 50 percent separate or divorce if a prison sentence is probable, before or even if actual incarceration never comes about (www.marriage.about.com).

and Effective Death Penalty Act of 1996 (A.E.D.P.A.) is surely one of the worst statutes ever passed by Congress and signed into law by a President." This should be abundantly clear to anyone who has studied the historical power of the Great Writ of Liberty.

ACTION ITEMS TO RESTORE HABEAS CORPUS

---

1. Repeal A.E.D.P.A. and Title 28 U.S.C. §§ 2254 & 2255 and mandate by law that the courts cannot judicially restrict this Constitutional right ever again.
2. Pressure state candidates to seek a Constitutional Convention to restore *habeas corpus,* and make support of repeal of all legislation restricting this constitutional right a litmus test for supporting any federal candidates.

The Charlie Engle Story

Frequently, after giving speeches or citing examples of injustice, I am asked, "So do you think *anybody* in prison is guilty?" The answer to this question is obviously yes, but the takeaway I hope the reader gets is how often government intentionally puts citizens in prison who don't belong there, and then refuses to do anything about it, even after that fact is proven.

Roughly three out of four persons currently incarcerated do not belong in prison, if actual innocence and/or a denial of due process during their convictions are counted as reasons for them not to be there. That is why I wrote this book, and that is why I believe it is so important.

I grew up in a family of lawyers and was married to a judge, but I had no idea what was going on until I began researching how and why America, the Land of the Free, had more people in prison than any country or society in human history. I began this investigation from within the system itself—I, myself, was in the American Gulag for seven years. When I learned how many of my fellow citizens were imprisoned there as well, I told myself that fact had to be wrong, but it was not.

During my living "experiment" as well as my research, it also became clear that those who make a living from this broken system have no intention of fixing it, never mind letting the people know what is being done in their name. A great deal of money is being made, and those within the system have mostly chosen willful blindness over working toward any meaningful reform.

The story of Charlie Engle is a perfect example of this phenomenon.

Who is Charlie Engle? He's a world-class athlete who ran across the entire Sahara Desert and is so famous for his physical feats that there was a movie made about him, titled *Running the Sahara*, narrated by Oscar-winner Matt Damon. He has also been ruined for life—even though it has been proven that Charlie was falsely accused by our judicial system—for a crime he did not commit.

Our government, on the other hand, has been proven to have committed multiple crimes against Charlie. Unfortunately, our system of American justice has given him no way to clear his name, or to force those in government who wronged him to pay a penalty for what they did.

United States v. Charles Engle has all of the elements of a thriller, just waiting for that "Perry Mason" moment where the guy runs in waving a sheaf of papers proving that Charlie did not do the crime.

The problem is, in our story, that moment actually happened. What failed to happen was the moment after that, when the judge is supposed to bang his gavel and set Charlie free while blasting the prosecutor for misconduct. In fact, even after it was proven beyond any reasonable doubt that the government—not Charlie—had lied and committed crimes, a total of six judges failed to free him. Justice may still work on TV, but it no longer works in the courts of America.

Joe Nocera of *The New York Times* wrote multiple articles about Charlie's story and this incredible miscarriage of justice, as did numerous other publications. However, our government remained and continues to remain blind, deaf, and most definitely dumb to its own systemic failures and foibles in this case.

FACTS: Charlie Engle was charged with making false statements on a mortgage application filled out by his broker while

Charlie was, in fact, completing his run across the Sahara. This impossible charge was actually a by-product of the film about his famous run—a film that also proved Charlie was not in America to see the application in question, for what was then known as a "liar loan." The government's own witness admitted at trial that the signature on the loan appeared to be forged, and Charlie's loan broker admitted to these forgeries. However, no one, including the prosecutor, told the jury or Charlie that someone else had already been convicted of the alleged crime. In fact, the information on the form was ultimately proven to be correct in every detail, so it's not entirely clear what "crime" government was alleging.

Despite this, Charlie's indictment, for all intents and purposes, became a conviction the day it was handed down from the grand jury, just like it does in 98.7 percent of all cases today. And with the destruction of defendants' rights by our courts and Congress, there was and is no means for Charlie to correct this injustice.

THE OUTCOME: Charlie's trial began on September 28, 2010. Sentencing took place on January 10, 2011. Charlie Engle spent two years at the Federal Corrections Institute, Beckley, West Virginia, and was ordered to pay $262,000 to a financial institution that was not named in the indictment and had no part in the transaction.

After reviewing the case, I filed a *habeas corpus* petition for Charlie Engle in 2011, requiring our government to prove how and why he was in prison. But due to the systematic gutting of this right, Charlie was denied a hearing—despite U.S. law, the Constitution, and 500 years of Anglo-Saxon jurisprudence requiring it.

Today, Charlie's case serves as a real-life example of why, if anything resembling justice is to be restored to our nation's judicial system, this constitutional right of *habeas corpus* must be returned to the people. Until this happens, no one in government is accountable, and its errors stand without any real or reasonable means of challenge.

THE CASE: Charlie's case began when an IRS agent, Robert W. Nordlander, was . . . reading a newspaper. That's the smoking gun. By his own admission in the grand jury transcripts, "Special Agent" Robert W. Nordlander (as he referred to himself throughout the trial) targeted Charlie for prosecution after reading an article about his historic run across the Sahara Desert to raise money for charity.

The article described how actor Matt Damon and Charlie had earned $6 million for a charity called H20 Africa from donations accrued during Charlie's grueling 111-day, 4,300-mile run across the Sahara's hostile sands—a feat never before (or since) accomplished by anyone.

H20 Africa used the funds to provide wells to hundreds of poor communities in the region that lacked dependable sources of clean water. Charlie went home tired and broke but happy. But as the old saying goes, "No good deed goes unpunished," and Special Agent Nordlander decided to make Charlie pay for what he had done . . . for charity.

Agent Nordlander was convinced that Charlie must have used the money for himself rather than giving it to the charity. He was also sure that somehow Charlie had avoided paying taxes on this money he never got. However, Agent Nordlander's own investigation proved the money raised had all gone to Matt Damon's charity, not Charlie. It showed that Charlie had committed no crime of any sort, and his taxes were all in order, meaning Agent Nordlander had wasted almost one year of his time and a significant amount of taxpayer money attempting to create a case against Charlie.

How could Special Agent Robert W. Nordlander explain this extraordinary waste of time and money to his superiors?

He could not. So he took the road so often traveled in such cases and lied to a federal grand jury. He told the grand jury, under oath, that Charlie earned "a negative $26,000" in income during the year in question. In truth, Charlie's income had been exactly what had been projected at midyear on the loan application ($180,000). Charlie could have cleared this discrepancy up himself; however, he was not invited to the grand jury hearing, which is another common practice today. Had the truth been revealed, it would have prevented an indictment.

Meanwhile, Assistant U.S. Attorney Joseph Kosky, the Eastern District of Virginia prosecutor, had already prosecuted and received admissions from 1) Charlie's loan broker, who admitted to forging his mortgage clients' signatures on their loan applications; 2) Charlie's bank officer, who had admitted to being in a conspiracy with the broker to get these loans through; and 3) the owner of the property for which Charlie traded in what is known as a 1031 exchange (named after the IRS code which makes it an approved method), who had also admitted to being in league with the broker and loan officer to do what they were now accusing Charlie of having done.

The fact that other people had already been convicted of these crimes proved that Charlie could not have committed them. However, this information, which would have exonerated him, was withheld from the jury and Charlie Engle's attorneys by Assistant U.S. Attorney Kosky. This was a violation of federal law.

Charlie was sentenced to federal prison for lying on a loan application he never saw and on which the information was correct in every detail. He was then ordered to pay $262,000 of "losses" to the Bank of America—which, even if Charlie Engle had given false information on the application, and even if he had signed it instead of the (convicted) loan broker, was still problematic.

First of all, there were no losses to recover. The funds paid out to Charlie Engle as part of a 1031 exchange were part of a swap. Under this section of the tax code, when one "swaps" for a higher priced property in a 1031 exchange, taxation is postponed until that property is sold. So Charlie was just getting back his own money from the new owner of the property, as opposed to a "loan." The *buyer* got a loan from the bank to pay Charlie, and Charlie paid off the old loan with those proceeds. The bottom line? Charlie Engle simply could not have caused any loss. He borrowed no money, and no bank lost any money on Charlie Engle.

Second, Bank of America was not even the bank that handled the transaction. That was Shore Bank of Cape Charles, VA. Bank of America's name never appeared on any paperwork, it was not named in or on the indictment, and its name did not appear even a single time in the transcripts of the trial. That is because Bank of America never made the supposed "loan" to Charlie Engle. It was not involved in any way, nor was it ever a party to any transaction at the point of closing or upstream.

So how is it that Charlie Engle was ordered by a court of law to pay this giant financial institution one-quarter of a million dollars?

That's a very good question—one which the courts of the United States have refused to answer for almost eight years at this writing.

The federal government dedicated a year of public resources, estimated at $650,000, to Special IRS Agent Robert W. Nordlander of North Carolina's investigation of a "crime" that Charlie Engle had not committed. The Office of the U.S. Attorney in Eastern Virginia spent close to $1 million in taxpayer money to convict Charlie Engle of something they knew, since their office had already convicted someone else of the crime, he had not done. Why did they go to such trouble and expense to imprison an innocent man?

The United States of America seems to have unlimited resources for prosecuting and imprisoning innocent citizens. Yet our nation offers no recourse where injustices committed by the courts against those citizens can be addressed, or those who committed these crimes can be brought to justice.

Every nation in the free world, with the notable exception of the United States, has an Office of Ombudsman dedicated to the purpose of providing its citizens with this type of recourse. However, when I recently suggested to a ranking member of the House Judiciary Committee that one should be established in every federal district, he just chuckled and said, "That will never happen."

Working on Charlie's case on our own, we were eventually able to force the judge who replaced the original judge who had allowed (or suborned) the errors in Charlie's case to revisit it and allow an appeal. By this time, Charlie had already served his sentence in full, and the Fourth Circuit Court of Appeals in Richmond, Virginia, gave him only days to collect his records, find counsel willing to assist him, and get an appeal filed by the date on its Order—giving one the sense that they did not want to review his case at all. Almost miraculously, attorney Randy James of Winston-Salem, North Carolina, was able to file it on time, but the appeal was immediately denied without review. The reason given for the denial surprised even me, though by then I thought I had seen it all.

The Appellate Court ruled that though Charlie had filed the petition exactly as its Order stated, the Court had intended to tell him to file it a day earlier. Since it was filed the day after the date they *meant* to tell him, the Court ruled that it was late and would not be heard, ever. Because, according to the Fourth Circuit Court of Appeals, Charlie should have known what they meant to say—as opposed to what they actually said.

So, now that he has been released from prison, Charlie Engle is saddled, for no discernable reason, with $262,000 in restitution to Bank of America.

U.S. Special Agent Robert W. Nordlander has paid no penalty for lying to the grand jury. Assistant U.S. Attorney Joseph Kosky has paid no penalty for his Brady violations (refusal to turn over evidence to the defense that someone else had already been convicted of the alleged crime). And of course, not one of the real criminals in the mortgage loan scandal have ever been charged, including the Bank of America executives who in large part caused the crisis.

Meanwhile, an American hero and world-famous runner is now removing dents from automobiles to pay Bank of America money that they never loaned him and with no means remaining in post-Constitutional America for Charlie Engle to be relieved of this burden.

CHAPTER 2

Repeal Laws

"The more laws, the less justice."

—*Marcus Tullius Cicero,*
Roman Statesman and Consul (106–43 BC)

These words were written more than 2,000 years ago. Yet they raise an important question for our current times: At what point do laws turn from rules by which society should live into tyranny? Human beings are born knowing right from wrong—we inherently know that taking the life of another, committing sexual assault, stealing what belongs to another, burning someone's property, and assaulting or defrauding another person are bad acts. These acts were also, until recent years, the extent of crimes for which Americans could be imprisoned.

Today, the United States has so many laws with prison as a penalty, and that number is growing so quickly, that no one actually knows how many exist. I asked the Chairman of the House Judiciary Committee and his staff during a meeting in August of 2015, and their guess as to how many *federal* laws carried the penalty of prison was off by over 300,000. If the men and women who are supposed to be in charge of the process don't know what is going on, we are really in trouble.

Our Founding Fathers were very clear on what the role of the federal government was to be in this arena. The

Constitution gives the federal government responsibility for the punishment of just three crimes—piracy, counterfeiting, and treason—and Amendment 10 clearly restricts them from going beyond these specific boundaries: "The powers not delegated to the United States by the Constitution, nor prohibited by it to the States, are reserved to the States respectively, or to the people." Leaving the bulk of the responsibility to the States or to the People was and remains the law. According to the Constitution, the States are solely responsible for making and enforcing all other laws, which they can tailor to their local cultures and mores.

So what is responsible for the massive federal government overreach that characterizes our legal system today? Some claim that the Commerce Clause in Article 1, Section 8 of the U.S. Constitution, which gives Congress the power "to regulate commerce with foreign nations, and among the several states, and with the Indian tribes," is to blame. However, this only gives the authority to regulate commerce, not to criminalize or punish it. And while this enables the government to regulate the states in the area of commerce, that authority does not extend to the people themselves.

Federalist Article (#45), which is credited to James Madison, the primary author of the Constitution, clearly defines the objectives and intention of where power should reside:

> The powers delegated by the proposed Constitution to the federal government, are few and defined. Those which are to remain in the State governments are numerous and indefinite. The former will be exercised principally on external objects, as war, peace, negotiation, and foreign commerce; with which last the power of taxation will, for the most part, be connected. The powers reserved to the several States will extend to all the objects which, in the ordinary course of affairs, concern the lives, liberties, and properties of the people, and the internal order, improvement, and prosperity of the State.

This article was written as a direct response to the anti-federalists, who worried that if the Constitution was approved, power would eventually concentrate in the hands of the central (federal) government and destroy the balance between the Nation and the States. This is precisely what has happened.

How far has this overreach now gone? As an example, Title 18, *Crimes and Criminal Procedures* alone now outlaws thousands of human behaviors. This body of law was passed during the Roosevelt Administration—more or less, because it never actually passed both houses of Congress. It was signed into law during a Senate recess by Roosevelt's vice-president, in violation of that body's Rules and Procedures.

While the Courts admit that Title 18 never legally became law, they have dismissed this argument from consideration, claiming that the laws *under* Title 18 were properly passed, so the fact that the entire overarching Title was not should not matter.

But it does matter—because the Constitution restricted the federal government to the punishment of just three crimes; piracy, counterfeiting, and treason. There was, therefore, no need for an entire body of criminal law and procedure, unless the Executive Branch intended to violate those constitutional provisions. This may be why the Senate refused to vote it into law in the first place, as the large percentage of constitutionalists in Congress during the Roosevelt administration would have likely viewed it as an overreach.

Claiming that an illegal body of law is acceptable simply because the laws passed under its umbrella were voted on—also in violation of law—is a rather large stretch, and likely indicates to any reasonable person that there was another agenda at play.

From the constitutional limit of punishing those original three federal crimes, Title 18 alone has outlawed 4,000 additional human behaviors. These behaviors were all, at one time, perfectly legal, but can no longer be performed without risk of imprisonment. They include such silliness as removing a tag from a pillow.

But Congress did not stop there. In fact, most American citizens in federal prison today are there for supposed violations of civil statutes, which are far outside of any authority the Constitution ever granted federal government. These statutes have now outlawed another 10,000-plus human behaviors, also with the punishment of prison, bringing us to more than 14,000 ways our federal government has essentially invented to punish its citizens with incarceration.

Congress then went on to create a lengthy slate of federal agencies—also not authorized in any way by the United States Constitution—and delegated its lawmaking authority to them. In the not-too-distant past, this would have been considered treason, which ironically *is* constitutionally punishable by the federal government.

To put this in perspective, suppose President George W. Bush decided to delegate his executive authority as the elected leader of the United States to Karl Rove, or to his Cabinet, so he could spend more time at his ranch in Texas? There would have been screams of outrage from every liberal think-tank and organization across our nation.

Now let's put this shoe on the right (conservative) foot. Suppose President Obama decided to delegate his executive authority as the elected leader of our nation to his friend and advisor, Valerie Jarrett, or even to Vice President Biden? All the players on the right would line up to scream bloody murder, demanding his immediate impeachment.

So how did Congress get away with delegating its responsibility, as our elected representatives, to unelected bureaucrats and heads of quasi-federal agencies—without any outrage from the public or our nation's media? These agencies, which are now making our laws, are referred to in the United States Federal Directory as "quasi-federal" specifically because they are not recognized or mentioned in the U.S. Constitution. Which should give us a hint as to their lawfulness, but that's beside the present point, which is: How did these unelected agencies get the power to make laws, and how many human behaviors have they turned into crimes?

No one knows for sure on either point, but the American Legislative Exchange estimates that unelected bureaucrats who were never authorized by the Constitution have outlawed another 300,000 human behaviors.

Allowing such things to happen isn't just unconstitutional, it's also dangerous. For example, 73 of these quasi-federal agencies have granted themselves the right to carry weapons, with powers to arrest citizens for violating their self-made laws, and kill those citizens should they resist. If that sounds too extreme to believe, try not paying your taxes for a few years and see what happens if you "resist" when the IRS comes to take your property.

Now let's return to our tally of laws, in light of Mr. Cicero's axiom that *more laws equal less justice.*

Title 18	4,000+
Civil statutes	10,000+
Other laws created by unelected bureaucrats	300,000+

The total is 314,000 human behaviors that were not even considered unlawful for most of this or any other nation's history, yet are now considered "criminal" in the Land of the Free, and are punishable by imprisonment. This shocking number of laws with prison as penalty is *many times* that of any other nation in human history.

In his 2009 book *Three Felonies a Day: How the Feds Target the Innocent*, Boston attorney Harvey Silverglate wrote that the average American now commits three federal felonies *every day* and doesn't even know it.[1] Many of these 314,000 laws are so vague, obscure or simply ridiculous that no person could

---

1 Harvey Silverglate, *Three Felonies a Day: How the Feds Target the Innocent* (New York: Encounter Books, 2011).

possibly know they were laws, or that they were breaking them. Even more disturbing, Mr. Silverglate also revealed that U.S. government attorneys tend to operate by choosing a target for prosecution first, then choosing which of the many laws available will be employed to convict and imprison that citizen.

Columnist George F. Wills explained how this works in his April 8, 2015 article, "When Everything Is a Crime." "In 2007, professor Tim Wu of Columbia Law School recounted a game played by some prosecutors. One would name a famous person— 'say, Mother Teresa or John Lennon'—and other prosecutors would try to imagine 'a plausible crime for which to indict him or her,' usually a felony plucked from 'the incredibly broad yet obscure crimes that populate the U.S. Code like a kind of jurisprudential minefield.' Did the person make 'false pretenses on the high seas'? Is he guilty of 'injuring a mailbag'?"

These are actual federal crimes for which a person can now go to prison, along with roughly 314,000 others, none of which are legally under the purview of federal government. Is it moral for a government to incarcerate a human being for such acts, ruining lives and families so frivolously?

The consequences are so widespread and so many lives have been affected that the public is finally becoming aware that this is happening. If our current elected officials continue to fail to do what is right and bring about change, the hope is that their constituents will vote them out of office and replace them with officials who are dedicated to righting this wrong.

As it stands, mass incarceration has emerged as a leading topic of the current political debate, and it is the only issue on which both sides of the aisle basically agree. Liberals are dismayed by the human cost of our mass incarceration epidemic in the form of shattered lives, families and communities, yet they continue taking donations from the prison industry and passing more laws in service to them. Conservatives are horrified by the cost of the prison industry ($80 billion each year, according to Attorney General Eric Holder) but also sycophantically serve those donors with votes. Libertarians are angry that the so-called Land of the Free has created 314,000 new reasons to restrict our freedom. Still, nothing is being done to rout out and eliminate its real cause, which is government overreach at all levels.

Returning to the Rule of Law is the answer.

If Cicero's axiom that more laws equals less justice is true, it can be taken one step further: The *most* laws equals the *least* justice. At some point, if there are more things that you can't do than things you can, you are no longer free

This is not a call for the elimination of all laws or punishments. It is simply a call for our government to also live by the law—specifically the U.S. Constitution—which requires that any rule under which We the People must live 1) be passed by an elected representative as opposed to an unaccountable delegate and 2) be passed and enforced by the proper level of government. This is not only the Law of the Land, it is also common sense.

At the closing of his article "The Plague of Overcriminalization,"[2] George Will summarized appropriately that "the scandal of mass incarceration is partly produced by the frivolity of the political class, which used the multiplication of criminal offenses as a form of moral exhibitionism." Anyone who has watched C-SPAN and seen politicians foaming at the mouth, screaming to an empty House of Representatives in the middle of the night in hopes of getting a few moments of airtime back home can easily understand Mr. Will's point. Soapbox posturing and frivolous lawmaking is doing real damage to our society, and it must come to an end.

Moving the passage and enforcement of laws closer to those who must suffer them only makes sense. It is far easier to put a state legislator out of his or her job for passing a bad law than

---

2 George Will, "The Plague of Overcriminalization," http://www.nationalreview
.com/article/394392/plague-overcriminalization-george-will.

it is to unseat a congressman who has been cemented into the Washington landscape.

Creating laws at the proper level of government is also a critical piece of the separation of powers between federal and state governments. At present, the federal government is in serious breach of its contract with both the States and the People, which should disturb both sides of the political divide. There is nothing "liberal" or "conservative" about mass incarceration, and it is unlikely to end until this balance of power is restored between the state and federal governments.

ACTION ITEMS TO REPEAL LAWS

---

1. Immediately decriminalize and/or repeal any federal law not specifically authorized as the purview of federal government in the United States Constitution.
2. Require each proposed law or statute to cite the constitutional provision under which its passage is authorized and how that act is not in violation of Amendment 10 of the Bill of Rights.
3. Require any statute with force of law to be directly passed, on the record, by members of the appropriate legislature before it can be applied.

The Brett Green Story

Brett Aaron Green studied art at the Savannah College of Art and Design until he ran out of money. He was a very talented young artist, but he was unable to afford to finish his studies. So he moved to Roanoke, Virginia, where he and his girlfriend Brittany ended up with the wrong crowd and started using drugs—first cocaine, then heroin.

One fateful night, high and looking for a place to sleep, they decided to crash in an empty home in the Preston Park community of Roanoke. No people were there, but plenty of guns were—over 2,500 of them, according to the police report. In their drug-induced haze, Brett and Brittany decided to try to turn a few of those weapons into money, and actually went door-to-door offering to sell them to the neighbors for cash.

It was stupid and illegal, to be sure—but there was no violence or threat of it, no one was hurt, and it was only minutes before the police were called and the duo was arrested. However, Brett will be paying for that crazy night forever. He may have only been sentenced to six years in prison, but the stigma of the Scarlet F will follow him for the rest of his life.

Brett's story is like that of so many Americans today. It's not a tale of an innocent person being punished for something he or she did not do. He was guilty beyond a shadow of a doubt, and he readily admits it. Instead, this story is about the human cost of America's "conviction machine."

Unless our country changes its system of lifetime punishment for minor, victimless crimes, Brett will be trapped in a life of menial labor, with no opportunity to develop his talents and become the person he could be. These are his own words about his situation, written a year after he was released from prison:

"Before I went to prison, I spent my life carelessly, no doubt. I was young and did not think about the consequences of things, until I paid the ultimate one. And I'm not talking about death—that's only one time. I speak rather of the shame and unreachable goals—a pair of consequences that greet me upon waking each morning and then put me to a worried sleep.

"Don't get me wrong. I don't want a pity party; I just want a fair shot at life. I made a very stupid mistake, and I admitted it, but my question to the powers that be is this—'How can that one mistake as a stupid kid define the remainder of my existence? Is that fair?'

"After prison, there is no such thing as a 'fair' anything. I've been turned down time and time again for excellent jobs, even when I was admittedly the best choice, for just one reason. They get this passionless look on their face and say, 'We're sorry, Mr. Green, but you have a record.'

" 'Ooooh, Like the 70 million other Americans just like me?' I want to say, but there is no use. Unless you've spent time in the meat grinder yourself, you don't know that it's the system that is broken far more than the people in it.

"I don't like or understand what is going on in this nation. I committed a mistake, not a crime like a real one. Nobody was murdered, raped, or harmed. We were messed up—in fact, we were so messed up that it should be obvious we would not have done something so stupid unless we were not ourselves. I sit here right now and cringe, thinking, 'How stupid!'

"But even though I did wrong, this system is wrong, too. Punishment is forever, and you just sink lower into Hell, day by stupid day.

"Drug problems are treated as a crime here rather than an illness like most civilized places, and I'm now forced to be a grunt for the rest of my life because of that stupid night. I can't even get into middle management, all because of a background check. 'We're sorry, Mr. Green, but you've got a record.' Yes, I know . . .

"I'll never be able to spread my wings and fly because of this system. Once it puts its claws in you, you are ruined forever.

"I don't like violence, but I would go to war for this country if it would just erase this blight on my name if I did so. Yes. I would risk losing my life if I could get back my life and have a chance to live it. But there is nothing I can do to change the system because they won't even let me vote for people who might do something about it. I just have to sit on the sidelines like the other 70 million Americans with a record, and watch.

"I can't even defend my home, my family or myself anymore, by law.

"How do they get away with ruining millions of lives forever, just for one stupid mistake?

"It is a terrific struggle just to get by every week. I own my name and I'll own what was done in it, but I also have a beautiful 12-year-old daughter who is now paying the price for my stigma as much as me. I can't get ahead enough to do things for her that might help her succeed. Is she to end up like I did? Maybe. I can't help her do better, because I have a 'record' and I can't do better.

"I don't know up from down these days.

"Wake up!!!!

"Every morning . . .

"I'm drinking myself to death.

"I am talented in many ways, but I'm not confident enough anymore to set that bird free and let it fly. This world has me sitting and waiting in the nest.

"This place scares me.

"What happens next? So many people I see, this isn't about me, it's what I bleed and nobody sees.

"This world is fucked, corrupt as a turnip picked by the strongest hand, that was directed by another man. You know what happens to a bird that tries to fly and falls?

"IT DIES.

"I feel lost most days. I'm willing to do the 9-to-5 work till my back breaks, 'cause that's all they've left for me to do. With this big Scarlet 'F' on my chest, what else can I do?

"In reality, the judge sentenced me to life, not just six years. I can never advance again in this country, and [I] am locked in to a future of mediocrity, at best. How is it that I am now to be judged for the rest of my life only by one night in my distant past rather than how I have performed and acted every day since?

"So though my sentence ended a year ago, I contend that I will be a prisoner for life, stuck in a menial position, judged by that stupid incident long ago rather than my abilities.

"I now understand why so many people actually become criminals when they are released from prison. That's about all that is left for them in a system bent on permanent punishment for even the smallest mistake, which prevents real rehabilitation forever."

Brett Green
December 10, 2015
Roanoke, Virginia

CHAPTER 3

Conduct Fair Prosecutions

"Better that ten guilty men escape than
that one innocent suffer."

—*Sir William Blackstone, 1765*

QUESTION: What happens to public prosecutors in the United States who intentionally violate the rights of those they indict, convict, and send to prison, or who knowingly break the law while acting in their official capacity?

ANSWER: Absolutely nothing.

The courts have granted our judges and prosecutors immunity, not by passing a law as legally required, but through their own judicial decisions. In other words, they have essentially gone outside the law and granted this immunity to themselves.

The only case in recent history in which a prosecutor suffered any penalty was the infamous Duke Lacrosse case in North Carolina in 2006, where Durham County, North Carolina, District Attorney Mike Nifong fabricated charges, falsified evidence, and encouraged lying by witnesses, all with a goal of putting innocent college students in prison to boost publicity during his bid for reelection.

As heinous as this sounds, the government did absolutely nothing to punish Mr. Nifong. Were it not for some courageous defenders who took on the system, he would almost certainly have escaped penalty for his crimes, like most corrupt judicial figures do today.

I do not use the word *courageous* lightly when referring to these defenders, as many who challenge the system today are punished severely for doing so. Despite this risk, attorney Kirk Osborn saw to it that Mr. Nifong was disbarred and removed from office, although this took years of time and international pressure to bring about. And even when Nifong was convicted, he was simply disbarred, and was not sent to prison for his crimes. Kirk Osborn died mysteriously shortly after the ruling.

Prosecutors today are not only immune from punishment for their crimes against citizens, there is also little if any oversight of their actions by anyone, and there are almost no records of the government responding to any wrongdoing on their part.

Fixing this problem is actually quite simple, and the answer lies in our own history. What was our founders' intention as far as holding our jurists to certain standards of conduct?

First of all, there was no such thing as a *public* prosecutor in colonial times. George Washington and Thomas Jefferson never heard of such an office and would likely have objected to such a concentration of power in one individual's hands.

In Washington's time, a professional attorney or other respected citizen was selected to represent the community against a person charged with an offense. A grand jury hearing was held to determine whether a crime had actually been committed, giving both sides a chance to present their case to 16 to 20 local citizens in an impartial, public, and open atmosphere. The defendant had the right to be present, as well as to present witnesses and evidence of his own, as guaranteed by the Sixth Amendment to the U.S. Constitution, just like the prosecutor and the person who had brought the charge of wrongdoing in the first place.

Prosecuting a case was a public service, performed infrequently at best, after which that attorney or individual returned to his normal life living and working in that same community. Therefore, the person chosen to represent the community as prosecutor had no interest in making an unfair case against a person. Making false claims against the innocent would make returning to that life difficult for a prosecutor, just as it would be difficult for a prosecutor who failed to protect the community from a dangerous person.

This provided the system with a natural balance of fairness—the accused was, for the most part, treated fairly, and the community was protected against truly bad or dangerous people. Prisons were few, and never full. At the federal level, there was no such a thing as a national prosecutor or U.S. Attorney, and there was no Department of Justice (nor was there a need for one under constitutional federal government) until it was created in 1871. The attorney general of the United States handled the few federal cases regarding piracy, counterfeiting, and interstate disputes. This worked very, very well, and America was known the world over for the fairness of its courts and juries.

This system persisted until the 1830s, when larger cities began creating offices of public prosecution as political posts. This had the effect of greatly consolidating government power over the courts, despite the fact that they were intended by our founders to be the province of "We the People," providing the bulwark and last line of defense *against* government.

And where are we today? According to the Department of Justice, "The United States Attorney system nationwide consisted of 94 headquarters offices and 138 staffed branch offices, as of the end of Fiscal Year 2010."[1] We've gone from one attorney general handling *all* federal cases to many, many thousands of aggressive attorneys, not including prosecutors, in every county of all 50 states.

---

1 http://www.justice.gov/sites/default/files/usao/legacy/2011/09/01/10statrpt.pd.

Grand jury hearings are now held in secret by public prosecutors without the defendant present to hear the evidence against them, and without counsel—violating both the Sixth Amendment's guarantee of a public process and the right to counsel. Behind those closed doors, all sorts of prosecutorial mischief takes place, including lies, overstatements, false witnesses, and fabricated evidence presented to a grand jury by a public prosecutor.[2]

In today's courts, an indictment is, in essence, a win. There is only a 5 out of 100 chance that the prosecutor will have to prove anything, ever, at a trial, as only one in 20 citizens are willing to face a deck so stacked against them. Meanwhile, prosecutors are encouraged to file as many federal cases against U.S. citizens as possible, and are compensated and promoted based on two factors: 1) How many convictions they get and 2) How many years in prison their targets are sentenced to. In the event that this sounds incredible to the reader, I am not only relying on articles such as those by George Will or admissions by public prosecutors who have been caught committing these crimes against the public, but by personal knowledge and interviews with corrupt former and present prosecutors who have come clean on how the system works today.

Today's public prosecutors are said to have the power to "indict a ham sandwich." Facing no penalty for lying to a grand jury, public prosecutors and U.S. Attorneys are free to present false evidence or put paid "witnesses" who are coached to provide false testimony on the stand. The truth is rarely told.[3]

---

2 This statement is the result of ten years of intensive research and assistance given in over 400 criminal cases, where the prosecutor gave misleading or one-sided presentations without the inclusion of exculpatory evidence; fabricated evidence, or staged false witnesses to garner the indictment. I have not reviewed or found a single case where a balanced or objective presentation was made by a public prosecutor, as intended by the nation's founders and the United States Constitution.

3 The main source of information on this systemic prosecutorial misconduct was former judge and U.S. Attorney Samuel T. Currin, from an interview

There is no longer a public process that involves the community at large at either the state or federal level. This is in clear violation of the Sixth Amendment, which states: "In all criminal prosecutions, the accused shall enjoy the right to a speedy and public trial, by an impartial jury of the State and district wherein the crime shall have been committed, which district shall have been previously ascertained by law, and to be informed of the nature and cause of the accusation; to be confronted with the witnesses against him; to have compulsory process for obtaining witnesses in his favor, and to have the Assistance of Counsel for his defence."

How prosecutors determined that the grand jury hearing, which initiates the process of a criminal prosecution (and is the *only* opportunity 95 percent of defendants today ever have to defend themselves), is not part of the criminal prosecution process not only violates the rights of the accused, it simply defies common sense. It is this absence of due process of law (and the absence of a penalty for those who violate the rights of defendants) that has created the mass incarceration crisis.

Of course, not every case that goes before a grand jury results in someone going to prison. However, those rare instances seem to be limited to cases of police officers shooting 12-year-olds

---

where I asked how the system became so corrupt—a position with which he totally agreed (after leaving office). He pointed to the basis for advancement and compensation of Assistant U.S. Attorneys as the cause, and he gave me these two elements as the sole criterion. When I asked why doing justice was not a criterion, he replied, "Anyone working in a U.S. Attorney's office trying to do the *right* thing, won't last a month. It's all about convictions and sentences, nothing else." Currin went on to admit that his office had paid informants to lie, taken family members as hostages to coerce pleas of guilt from their targets, falsified evidence, and fabricated evidence in whole part. "We did anything and everything to win. That was all that mattered."

and other unarmed citizens, or cases involving other alleged crimes by officers and officials within our government.

I recently interviewed a federal grand jury chairman in North Carolina, Eric Bradsaw, who served in that position for one year. I asked him how many out of the hundreds of cases presented by the U.S. Attorney's office over the course of that year did not result in an indictment. His answer to the question? "None."

And the indictment is just the beginning. The prosecutors then do whatever is necessary to prevent their targets from being free to prepare an adequate defense, which frequently leads to more inappropriate conduct. While they may not be legal, these tactics are successful in the vast majority of cases. According to the Department of Justice Bureau of Statistics, in 2008, 77.1 percent of those accused by our government were never free for even a single day between being arrested and going to prison.

That does not, however, mean the span of time between arrest and conviction is usually brief. Though federal law (18 U.S.C. §3161, et seq.) requires defendants to be tried within 70 days (absent a short list of "excludable delays"), prosecutors rarely live by this law either, nor have I seen one suffer a penalty for illegally holding a citizen beyond the required date for release. Yet there is no oversight and no penalty for misconduct—something prosecutors are clearly aware of.

In fact, while Federal Statute 18 U.S.C. §3162(a)(2) states, "Failure of the defendant to move for dismissal prior to trial or entry of a plea of guilty or nolo contendere shall constitute a waiver of the right to dismissal under this section," meaning complete dismissal of an indictment is required if the prisoner or his attorneys files a motion for dismissal after 70 days, today attorneys in certain districts are actually sanctioned by judges if they follow this law.[4] So they rarely use it, *even*

---

4 This is now policy in the Federal District Court of Western North Carolina and others, as confirmed by attorneys who have been threatened by federal judges for filing motions to enforce these laws.

though it is the law. Millions of citizens go to prison unnecessarily, simply because their attorneys were too timid to file the motion, or they did not know the law in the first place. Either case amounts to ineffective counsel and should result in an overturn of any subsequent conviction, but that also rarely happens.

I have worked on many cases where un-convicted or innocent citizens were held in dangerous county jails for five years or longer, simply because they refused to plead guilty to a crime. Prosecutors use this type of illegal incarceration to force guilty pleas and avoid trials. And it works—statistics show 97 percent of citizens who are indicted are eventually pressured into pleading guilty through the use of coercive tactics by prosecutors, and often by their own attorneys. This means that in America today, an indictment by a grand jury, for all intents and purposes, is a conviction. The overall percentage of those who are found guilty, including the handful who risk going to trial, is 98.7 percent.

Is it any wonder that the United States now has the highest conviction rate in the world? A dearth of due process of law, combined with unconscionable misconduct by prosecutors (and judges), has rigged the game. As in gambling, over time, the house always wins.

Another factor weighing against indicted citizens is the fact that most of them can't afford to go to trial. The staggering cost of defending against a charge, especially at the federal level, is beyond the means of all but the wealthiest of Americans, while the government has comparatively unlimited funding. This insures that the less than three percent of defendants who eventually do go free are, in almost every case, among the extremely wealthy. Which in turn ensures that our prisons are populated by the poor and minorities.

A recent *Forbes* article provided a partial list of what some citizens (guilty and innocent) recently spent to defend themselves. The article stated, "It was estimated that Raj Rajaratnam spent over $40 million to defend himself against charges of insider trading. After a 9-week trial and 6 days of jury deliberations, Rajat Gupta, who is currently having his legal fees paid by Goldman Sachs (former Board Member), was also found guilty and was sentenced to 2-years in prison. He is free pending appeal."

"Another high-profile case was that of Bill Ruehle, CFO at BroadCom, who successfully defended himself on charges that he backdated stock options. Ruehle told me in an interview that the legal tab, paid for by BroadCom, was in the tens of millions of dollars. So what does it cost mere mortals to defend themselves when the Feds come knocking? A lot."[5]

You can't beat the house when they have all the chips and can rig the game without penalty. You can take them on—with the odds still against you, no matter what the truth is—and wind up with an even longer sentence while bankrupting your family (or business). Or you can give up and take your new prison number. Most choose the latter course of action. Which is why, according to the BNA *Criminal Law Reporter*, "The U.S. Department of Justice estimates that 71 million people—approximately 25 percent of the American population—have a criminal record."[6]

As democratic Senator (and former 2015 presidential candidate) Jim Webb wrote in an article for *Parade* magazine back in 2010, "Either we are the most evil people on earth, or we are doing something very wrong."

What does this admission by the U.S. Department of Justice, that one in four Americans around you every day now has a "criminal" record, actually mean? Think about it the next time you are in a place of worship, at a movie theater, watching a

---

5 Walter Pavlo, "The High Cost of Mounting a White-Collar Criminal Defense," May 30, 2013, forbes.com.
6 BNA *Criminal Law Reporter*, May 19, 2010 (Vol. 87, No.7).

ballgame, or just driving down the highway. Look around you. One of every four people you see has a criminal record and has lost his or her rights as an American citizen, according to the Department of Justice (and *because* of that Department of Justice, in many cases).

How can a nation claiming to be free or purporting to have a fair and equitable system of justice have one in every four of its citizens disenfranchised and labeled a "felon"? This cannot possibly occur in a system that is fair and equitable, where the laws being enforced are reasonable and their adjudication is above board. There is simply no defense for a nation that disenfranchises one quarter of its people.

How did we get to this terrible place? It began with the acts described in Chapters One and Two; the 1996 decision in which Congress took away our constitutional right to challenge this sort of wrong-doing through *habeas corpus,* and the passage or authorization of hundreds of thousands of laws, with prison as a penalty, that are so vague, few people could even know they were breaking them.

A third factor is the near-elimination of an ancient concept known as *mens rea,* which was once an element of any criminal prosecution or law. The central question of *mens rea* was, "Did the person *intend* to do wrong?" Unless the prosecutor could prove to a jury that there was criminal intent on the part of the defendant, there could be no conviction. But today, Congress and its delegate lawmakers no longer require *mens rea* as an element of guilt in most recent statutes and regulations.

So we have public prosecutors with unlimited authority to indict whomever they please for over 314,000 separate human behaviors, most of which have never before in history been in violation of law. We have several thousand public prosecutors who can now indict whomever they want, whenever they want, and convict them using less-than-lawful methods (without penalty). Furthermore, we have a host of questionable quasi-federal agencies now assisting these prosecutors by feeding them cases for prosecution. They make laws and their agents enforce them, arresting and imprisoning whomever they've targeted.

Every day, law-abiding American citizens fall prey to this miasma, and it is all happening outside of Constitutional authority. So what do we do now?

First, we must retrace our steps back to Rule of Law and the Constitution and restore the grand jury to its original design and purpose. No more closed doors. No more secret sessions where lies can be told by false witnesses without challenge or confrontation by the accused. No more one-sided presentations without truthful evidence or inclusion of exculpatory facts to provide balance and truth and the accused is not allowed to have counsel.

Second, we need to return to the original grand jury system, where an attorney or citizen at large is chosen to represent the community rather than a hired gun. *Public* prosecutors who thrive only on convictions and lengthy sentences have proven to be a very, very bad idea. These permanent positions allow dangerous amounts of (political) power to collect in a very few hands.

Instead, why not call on the 1.22 million attorneys currently practicing in the United States, with 44,000 new law degrees being issued each year? There are plenty of attorneys who can be enlisted, as they once were, for this public service. With an average of about 50,000 per state, they might wait years to ever get a case, so there would certainly be no substantial burden on them. Any member of the bar, regardless of type of practice or training, should be subject to this required public service. One does not need training in criminal practice or procedure to present evidence objectively to his or her neighbors, which is all the job is supposed to require.

If we simply follow the law and return to this way of doing things, the number of indictments will plummet, and the rate of

conviction will return to a fair percentage. The rotating prosecutors will no doubt be anxious to get their public service
over with as soon as possible and get back to their day jobs.
The defendants will not be left to languish in county jails for
months and years, and will be tried as the law and Constitution
intended, within 70 days, and will be released on bond to prepare for trial as Amendment 8 demands—because the attorney
enlisted to represent the community has no incentive to cause
a delay or coerce an improper outcome.

If only a few states were to return to this constitutional,
working system, it would give the rest of the nation an opportunity to see how well it works. Once the cost savings and the
rapid return to real justice become apparent, citizens of other
states will quickly demand that their legislatures follow suit—
regardless of how much the prison industry is donating to their
political campaigns.

In the meantime, it's time to get rid of prosecutorial immunity.
There is no difference between a public prosecutor knowingly
indicting an innocent citizen and holding him or her in jail for
years, and any other common criminal kidnapping someone
and holding them in their basement—except that one gets a
raise and the other gets the electric chair. Public prosecutors
at the state or federal level who are found to have violated the
rights of their targets, presented false or misleading evidence
to a grand or petit jury, withheld exculpatory evidence, or
in any way been determined to have violated due process of
law should be disbarred, and—if there was *mens rea* in their
crime against the People—sent to prison. That is where they
belong, as they are a real menace to society—unlike most of
the 71 million American citizens these prosecutors have sent
there before them.

ACTION ITEMS FOR FAIR PROSECUTIONS

1. Restore the grand jury to its historical function as an open, public affair, eliminate "public" prosecutors, and require all members of the local bar association to rotate as acting prosecutors as part of their obligation to the public.
2. Remove any immunities or protections for public prosecutors for crimes committed against defendants or in cases involving the violation of their rights.

The IRP6 Story

Imagine for a moment that you have finally returned home after serving the United States government as a cryptographic systems analyst at NORAD (North American Aerospace Defense Command). You have a top secret clearance. You know things that you can never reveal, even to your family. But you have also witnessed enormous flaws in America's defenses, from the nation's highest vantage point within government.

The good news, however, is that your friends are working on a software product to help fix these flaws, and they want you to join the team. After the 9/11 tragedy, you and your friends, who are experts in the information technology field, exchange ideas on how to further innovate the software to solve the type of information sharing failures that contributed to the horrifying attack on the Homeland in 2001.

Together you create the Investigative Resource Planning Company (IRP), and with these five close friends and experts, you build a type of software that can accurately detect threats to cities and nations before attacks occur, giving law enforcement authorities a chance to prevent them.

Your product, Case Investigative Life Cycle (CILC), is built and tested. It is demonstrated to various government organizations, including the Department of Homeland Security. They repeatedly test your product and, on numerous occasions, request you to come to Washington, D.C., from your base in Colorado Springs. The New York City Police Department also reviews your program and decides it is of great interest. IRP partner

David Banks later said, "We were 100 percent convinced that CILC was the only product of its kind and could revolutionize the way law enforcement manages and shares information."

Homeland Security apparently sees this too, and recommends retraining retired federal agents to help flesh out the program to meet their needs.

New York City Police Department's commanding officer of the Investigative Liaison Unit, John Shannon, serving under Police Commissioner Raymond Kelly, describes the IRP program as *the best investigative management solution he has ever seen*, and says his department intends to "close a deal with IRP in 2004."

DHS (Department of Homeland Security) also has your product put into its 2004 budget projections for the following year, and earmarks $12 million for the New York Division of Immigration and Customs Enforcement division as the place to start live testing.

Senator Ben "Nighthorse" Campbell offers to be a reference for the product and company after reviewing it and recommends recently retired federal agents who can help put a federal face on CILC. The program is even modified at the request of DHS to include agencies under its umbrella (Secret Service, Border Patrol, Coast Guard)—a process so intense that, in late 2004, you have to outsource work through staffing agencies to meet the requirements.

You and your partners are hardly able to contain your enthusiasm. You have the solution that can close your nation's security gaps—and DHS and the NYPD are on board. After all your hard work, success is just around the corner.

But then, on February 9, 2005, a small army invades your office. They burst in screaming obscenities and commands. They order you and your employees into the company's break room and hold you hostage for 11 hours while they attempt to copy your proprietary software product and all of the backup for its development.

In other words, they simply try to steal what they were supposed to buy within a few weeks.

Every time you try to ask what they are doing, you are ordered by men with guns to stay still and quiet in the break room of your own offices. Thoughts race through your head. *Do they just want to see what we have before they actually buy it? If so, why didn't they just ask? Are they scared some foreign nation will buy our software first? We would never do that! Is this some racist thing because most of the IRP partners are black?* (According to the partners, the agents only frisked the black employees and partners and ordered them to be searched, never touching the white employees.)

You know in your heart that you have done nothing wrong, so it certainly cannot be about you or your partners. However, something is very, very wrong with what is going on. And as the hours crawl by, you begin to question your assumptions.

Is this the same country that we served so honorably and selflessly? This was the kind of behavior we volunteered to fight against. This is not supposed to happen in America. You have all day and well into the night to think of these things while you watch American "justice" unfold before your eyes.

It runs through your mind that you and your partners have pledged everything you have to make this program work, and owe quite a bit of money to the companies hired to finish the alterations demanded by the same government that just stormed your office and stole everything. What could this possibly be about, and why are they doing this?

Fast-forward a few years. You and your partners have all been charged in federal court. The government was never able to find anything wrong, but the Office of the U.S. Attorney has claimed to the court that your company has been shut down because you owe your contractors money. Of course, this is now true. But the reason you can't pay your bills is that the government decided to steal everything they could rather than purchase it. They also poisoned your pending contracts by contacting your customers and claiming your company was "under criminal investigation." They wound up so completely gutting your company that you were unable to even hire attorneys for your defense.

The government clearly doesn't have a case. But the Office of the U.S. Attorney is very careful to make sure that the judge is on board to help him get his conviction. When the original federal grand jury refuses to indict (a rarity today), another grand jury is handpicked to do so.

Why was our government so bent on destroying these innocent people who were helping our nation? No one is sure (yet), but the facts are that 1) the United States government stormed the IRP offices and took or copied everything they could (when their warrant only listed financial records) and 2) the company that developed the software (IRP) was destroyed by the U.S. government, and the partners and developers were sent to prison for a long, long time.

The partners—patriotic Americans, most of whom had defended their country or been in its service—decided to go to trial, believing that justice would prevail. Unable to afford counsel because government had destroyed their business and incomes, but unwilling to accept the inferior lawyers the government offered them, the IRP 6 acted as their own counsel.

At the beginning of the trial, the government's judge, Christine M. Arguello, ordered the six to testify against themselves and each other, which is illegal. In essence she told them, "Help us find a way to incriminate you, or I'll send you all to jail for contempt of court anyway."

This was in violation of Amendment Five of the U.S. Constitution and voided the trial. Since everyone present in the courtroom heard Judge Arguello openly order it, the defendants immediately ordered a copy of the transcript to prove that their rights had been violated and void the trial. But Judge Arguello refused to allow them to have a copy of the transcript of their own trial—which is another violation of federal law.

She has continued to refuse to provide a transcript for their appeal, which has kept them all in federal prison.

I become involved with the IRP 6 through the radio show "A Just Cause," which was inspired by their injustice, and is based in Colorado Springs, Colorado, where their families now live without them.

Judge H. Lee Sarokin, U.S. Court of Appeals (3rd Cir.) retired, was asked to summarize this case for us after reviewing it, to add a more objective voice in this story's telling. Judge Sarokin wrote:

> In a federal court in Colorado, 5 experienced, educated African-American executives (defending themselves) were ordered by a judge to testify in violation of their constitutional right against self-incrimination. When one commenced testifying and another objected, the judge denied giving any such instruction. The defendants demanded that the transcript of the judge's statement be furnished. The trial continued; the defendants were convicted and sentenced to 7 to 11 years; the convictions were affirmed and review denied by the Supreme Court. *To this day the transcript of that conversation has never been provided* [Emphasis is original].
>
> An FBI raid was conducted on their business and everything seized, thus making it impossible for them to fulfill their obligations which they assert they had always intended to honor. Thereafter, upon a complaint received from a staffing company, the head of the local FBI responded that it was a civil not a criminal matter and declined to investigate further. Nonetheless, the charges were later submitted to a grand jury, which refused to indict. But someone (unbeknownst to the defendants) apparently persisted in having the matter submitted and another grand jury finally indicted—some years after the first letter of complaint.
>
> At the trial, the government conceded that the defendants made no money as a result of the alleged scam. Also, it is

difficult to reconcile the charge with the time and money devoted to the project by the defendants and the unanswerable questions: Why would scammers pick law enforcement as their target? Why would they personally guarantee the obligations to the staffing companies? How could they possibly make any money unless the program were a success and contracts obtained? Who pushed so hard for the indictments?

And finally there is the treatment of the defendants—unusually long sentences—denied bail pending appeal as flight risks. None have any criminal records. They all belonged to the same church and lived in the same community. They and their families are replete with service in the armed forces and a long history of such service. They have families. White executives who have supervised or directed conduct that has resulted in death of consumers and employees are not even charged, and yet these 5 African-Americans (and one white colleague) are pursued relentlessly and punished harshly for basically the failure to pay corporate debts.

As of this writing, the IRP6 are still falsely imprisoned, and Judge Christine M. Arguello refuses to turn over the transcript of the trial to prevent them from having the opportunity to file a proper appeal which would, by law, require them to be released or retried.

CHAPTER 4

Limit Plea Bargaining

TABLE 3: Average Sentence, Number and Percent for Federal Drug Defendants by Plea/Trial (FY 2012)

	Sentence	Number of Convictions	Percentage of Convictions
Plea	5 years, 4 months	24,018	97.0%
Trial	16 years	747	3.0%

Source: Human Rights Watch analysis of United States Sentencing Commission FY 2012 Individual Datafiles, http://www.ussc.gov/research-and-publications/commission-datafiles/index.cfm.

Another symptom of the disease plaguing our justice system is plea bargaining—a practice that, according to our Constitution, is actually illegal. As the chart above indicates, roughly 97 percent of cases in America are now settled by this process, because few defendants are willing to risk going to court with the deck so heavily stacked against them. All the winning cards are held firmly in the government's hand.

Why are so many un-convicted citizens giving up their right to face a jury of their peers? There are several reasons, beginning with the fact that sitting in a dangerous, overcrowded county jail, locked away from the world, there is simply no way for a defendant to adequately prepare for trial. However, it's standard practice for prosecutors to do everything possible to make sure their targets are denied bail, successfully keeping more than three-quarters (77.1 percent, according to the U.S. Department of Justice) of them behind bars from the moment of their arrest until they are sent to prison.

After spending months or even years in these dirty, dangerous facilities, un-convicted citizens become so desperate to get out that they will do anything—including going to prison, since detainees quickly learn from their peers that even prison is better and safer than county jails and privately owned lock-ups.

A strong indicator of the desperation of these un-convicted detainees is their rising suicide rate, as highlighted recently by the Sandra Bland case in Texas. Ms. Bland was in the midst of moving from Chicago to Texas to start a new job when she was pulled over for failing to properly signal while changing lanes. Ms. Bland is seen on video asking the officers why they have pulled her over, and is then seen being arrested and handcuffed—all because of an alleged minor traffic violation. And even that violation was in question, as Ms. Bland claimed she only pulled over to let the fast-approaching cruiser with lights flashing and sirens blaring pass her.

Of course, the deputies didn't pass Ms. Bland, and likely did not intend to, as this tactic is commonly used to create an incident when sheriffs want to stop someone.

A few days later, Sandra Bland hung herself in jail. She decided to take her life, rather than wait and see what our system of justice would deliver next. And she was not alone. The suicide rate of un-convicted U.S. citizens in county jails is over three times that of the rest of the population, compared to a slight uptick in the suicide rate among people in prison.

Why is this happening? County jails are incredibly dangerous, disease-ridden places that are virtually useless in terms of protecting the public. According to my research and experience, habitual criminals who plead guilty often receive reduced sentences and return to the streets, putting the public in real danger, while the innocent are held in jail until they agree to admit to committing a crime.

As for the innocent citizens left behind, the U.S. Department of Justice has finally revealed the truth about the conditions they face. "Allen J. Beck, the senior BJS statistician who has been the lead author on all of these studies, tells us the new findings indicate that nearly 200,000 people were sexually abused in American detention facilities in 2011."[1]

The situation is even worse for juveniles, who are now locked up indiscriminately by prosecutors and courts with adults. "The new studies confirm previous findings that most of those who commit sexual abuse in detention are corrections staff, not inmates. That is true in all types of detention facilities, but especially in juvenile facilities. The new studies also confirm that most victims are abused repeatedly during the course of a year. In juvenile facilities, victims of sexual misconduct by staff members were more likely to report eleven or more instances of abuse than a single, isolated occurrence."[2]

In addition to the very real chance of being sexually abused (22 percent of all who have been in jail or prison), there's also the problem of nonsexual violence. In detention facilities like these, murderers, rapists, pedophiles and the most violent among us are randomly mixed with the innocent, the timid, the weak, and the young. As many as nine bodies and injuries came out of one 54-man housing pod in Charlotte, North Carolina, in just one day in 2006[3]—yet not one of those men had been convicted of the crime for which they were accused. Under the law, they were still innocent, yet they paid the ultimate penalty.

In addition, diseases like HIV, AIDS, and MRSA run rampant—nowhere in the United States are these illnesses

---

1 http://www.nybooks.com/articles/2013/10/24/shame-our-prisons-new
   -evidence/.
2 Ibid.
3 The Mecklenburg County Jail.

more concentrated than in our jails and prisons, because that is where government now houses its drug users, sexual deviants, and mentally ill. As a result, one un-convicted citizen (on average) died every month from abuse, violence, disease, or neglect in this Charlotte, North Carolina jail, while I was illegally held there.

Meanwhile, the government continues to release the truly violent back to the streets, as it did in the well-known case of FBI informant Whitey Bulger. Bulger was kept from going to jail for very serious crimes in exchange for his agreement to act as an informant for the FBI. While performing this service and living under the government's protection, Bulger murdered 19 people. The FBI knew it, the government turned a blind eye, and the U.S. Attorneys in Boston ignored it, because Bulger was giving them high-profile cases and convictions by informing on his competitors.

When other law enforcement agencies began to investigate Bulger and the FBI could no longer protect him, his handler, FBI Agent John J. Connolly, Jr., warned him to flee.[4] Ultimately he was arrested, and in August of 2013, he was convicted of 11 of the 19 murders he committed while being under FBI protection as their snitch.

Whitey Bulger may be an extreme example, but the Whitey Bulger *system* is at work in every county jail across America, thanks to public prosecutors who set criminals free to help them get more convictions. They give their own Whitey Bulgers a pass on punishments in exchange for helping create cases and testifying against others—though often, like Bulger, they are never even asked to testify against anyone—just to provide questionable often unreliable information.

This snitch system has become epidemic as a result. Prosecutors routinely exchange leniency (or turning a blind eye to criminal activity, like the FBI did with Whitey Bulger), for

---

4 http://www.nytimes.com/interactive/us/bulger-timeline.html?_r=0.

knowingly false testimony from jailhouse informants and criminals returned to the street.

In fact, the more innocent a citizen in county jail happens to be, the less likely he or she is to be freed on bail. Of course, holding an un-convicted citizen for longer than 90 days without bail is also very much against federal law. 18 U.S.C. § 3164(c) demands that the conditions of bail for any citizen not tried within 90 days must be set, regardless of the crime. However, I have never seen this law followed by the prosecutors and courts at either the state or federal level for anyone claiming to be innocent. While for the guilty, bail is common.

Clearly, "pre-trial detention" is not being used to protect the public, as the Bulger case has proven, but to force the innocent to admit to committing a crime while quite often letting the Whitey Bulgers go back to the street. This despite the fact that holding these citizens beyond 90 days, guilty or not, is in direct violation of § 3164(c) of the Federal Criminal Code and everything for which our justice system once stood.

No one is guilty until proven so at trial—at least that is the law.

Some state attorneys and judges have argued that they are not required to follow this federal statute, but the words of Article 6 of the U.S. Constitution make it quite clear that they are: *"This Constitution, and the Laws of the United States which shall be made in the Pursuance thereof . . . shall be the Supreme Law of the Land; and the Judges in every State shall be bound thereby . . ."*

Holding prisoners without trial after 70 days, or over 90 days with certain delays, is a federal crime. The judges and prosecutors who violate this federal law should pay a penalty for breaking it.

Only then will this odious practice cease.

Simply enforcing the law against those in our government who break it on a routine, if not daily, basis, is the short answer to fixing the problem of mass incarceration. But there

is no official or agency presently willing to force public prosecutors and judges to follow the law, and no meaningful means
of challenging their lawlessness.

The system of plea bargaining that has developed under
these conditions is as simple as it is inhumane. The accused
are charged and held until they agree to "voluntarily" admit
to committing a crime. The judges hold a colloquy where they
require the citizen to state under oath that they are "voluntarily" pleading guilty to a crime, and that they are satisfied
with the attorney who allowed them to be violated.

This is a scam worthy only of third-world nation. No person
who is unlawfully imprisoned can be said to "voluntarily"
plead guilty to anything, and no attorney that allows it, as
most now do, can be anything but a shill for the prosecution.

The really criminal part of this horrible system is, as part of
the plea agreement, the prosecutor now requires the citizen to
waive his or her right to challenge their lawlessness. He or she
must swear to allow the violations of law and Constitution
committed by the prosecutor and court to go unchallenged,
though it is those same violations which led to the defendant
giving up on justice and taking the deal in the first place.

That is the essence of "plea bargaining," and as long as it is
allowed to continue, any hope of our nation recovering from
its mass incarceration crisis is an empty one.

There is nothing wrong with a truly guilty person, without
pressure, promise, or threat from the prosecutor, choosing to
admit guilt to a crime on their own (within the 70-day period
allowed for trial). Throwing a citizen in jail, threatening additional charges and prosecution if they don't plead guilty, using
jailhouse snitches who are seeking time-cuts as "witnesses" to
force confessions, while illegally imprisoning the defendant in
a dangerous, overcrowded environment, however, is not right,
moral, or constitutional. It is a complete denial of due process,

and it happens every day in every district across the entire nation that I have studied (including all thirteen Federal Districts and most states except Alaska and Hawaii, as I have not personally worked on any cases in those states).

The Constitution demands a trial by jury of anyone charged with a criminal offense, and we should return to that means of determining guilt or innocence. Allowing government to break the law to coerce a plea of guilt and then force the victim of such abuse to waive his or her rights and protections against such criminal conduct under color of law can no longer be tolerated. Any violation of the defendant's substantial rights or statutory protections must be allowed as basis for overturning a conviction or plea deal at any time during or after the process.

There is no such thing as harmless error when it comes to violating a citizen's constitutional rights. Not only is the citizen harmed by such lawlessness, but the system itself suffers greatly. Government's penalty for breaking the law during its prosecutions must be the voiding of its victim's conviction. If government's prosecutors, agents, or judges violate due process, federal law, or the United States Constitution in the process, a conviction by that process can no longer be allowed to stand.

And no *waiver* of such illegal behavior by our government can be tolerated any longer. There must be zero tolerance of government crime in the criminal justice process if the United States is ever again to have a justice system where actual *justice* can be expected as the outcome. Perhaps then our government's error rate might drop below 73 percent.

If Congress finds the political will to end America's mass incarceration crisis (rather than supporting it), it can do so in one simple act. Pass a law that any prisoner not legally prosecuted by government according to protections in the law and U.S. Constitution must be released immediately. Our nation's prisons would empty in a hurry.

ACTION ITEMS FOR LIMITING PLEA BARGAINING

1. Congress must overtly outlaw pre-trial detention by government at any level, beyond the limits expressed in federal law.
2. The penalty for the government's violation must be the dismissal of indictment or any subsequent conviction, with prejudice.[5]
3. Plea agreements that require waivers of constitutional rights beyond that of not having a trial must be voided as a matter of law.
4. Trial by jury must be held in every case where a criminal charge has been made, as required by the Sixth Amendment, unless the defendant has requested, in writing, to plead guilty without waiver of rights (except trial), and has done so within 70 days after arrest or indictment.

---

5 "With prejudice" means that the dismissed charges cannot be brought against the citizen again, otherwise, there is no real penalty for government prosecutors. They can simply reindict.

The Chester Ray Williams Story

How Chester "Chet" Williams avoided being a politician, maybe even president, is beyond me. A more affable, entertaining soul has rarely been born.

With an instant ability to charm, this well-educated rodeo cowboy, singer, songwriter, high school teacher, master welder, and West Texas guitar player seems to have everything.

Unfortunately, "everything" also now includes a federal record. He can't get a job. The Great State of Texas barred him from even getting a driver's license for a year after his release. Today, at age 63, he's not quite sure what to do.

This despite the fact that his conviction for "attempt to conspire to obtain marijuana" has been overturned. Why? Because there is no such law. However, this fact did not bother the prosecutor in El Paso or Federal Judge Frank Montalvo when they sent him to prison—all because this old cowboy refused to lie for them. The way they saw it, Chet had to go to prison for something, even if no law existed under which they could send him. Now this fine man has been ruined, as no one has seen fit to remove his "record," which remains in every database in the country.

Here is Chester Ray William's story:

After a few decades riding the rodeo circuit as a team-roping Champ at U.S.T.R.C. and World-Series events, Chet's knees started giving out—especially the right one. He had tried teaching high school and was great at it, but he missed the road after a few years in Seattle and went back to being a cowboy.

He knew he had more years behind him on the rodeo circuit than there probably were ahead. There had been too many falls and rollovers by 500 pound steers—even a tough man like Chester Ray Williams could only take so much. He knew his knees wouldn't last much longer, however, he could not afford the surgery he needed.

Chet made the decision to go into real estate and get his license in West Texas. There was a boom going on, and his goal was to make some money for retirement by getting in on it. But before he could start, while he was on his way home from what might have been his last rodeo, an old friend called and offered Chet a chance to make some money on a real estate investment.

The friend said that he had some land, already sold at a nice profit, provided he could just get the down payment to secure the deal. If Chet would loan him $15,000, it would be doubled in a few weeks and repaid. Chet figured that extra $15,000 would give him just enough to live on while he got his real estate license—in addition to the $37,000 he'd saved from his rodeo winnings and odd welding and other jobs. Chet agreed to meet his friend at a restaurant and loan him the $15,000 for the deal. That's when life as Chet knew it ended.

When he pulled into the restaurant parking lot, he was approached by two men asking if he wanted to buy marijuana. Chet declined and told them he was just meeting an old friend, at which point, out of nowhere, agents swarmed him and his truck. They arrested Chet, expecting to find some criminal item in the (illegal) search, but couldn't. They spent an hour picking through everything he had, including his rodeo winnings bag, where he had the cash from his welding jobs and rodeo riding to loan his friend, plus just enough to live on while getting through the real estate course.

Chet was questioned, frisked, questioned again, shaken down, questioned once more, and finally, having found no crime, no drugs, and not even a missing taillight, the agents arrested him for "transportation of a large sum of money."

Chet later learned that the setup was actually a sting and he was expected to say "yes" to the marijuana question. His friend had not been entirely candid about the "investment opportunity," and traded the information about their meeting for leniency when he got busted—at least that's our best guess as to what really happened.

The agents apparently assumed Chet knew what his friend was up to and agreed to get involved, so they set up the entrapment scheme to try to make a sale. But it didn't work. Chet was not interested.

Regardless of the facts, they seized his cash on the spot and let him go. Having worked on many similar cases, I am convinced that if Chet had allowed them to keep his money without protest—as happens in almost every such case of seizure—his story would end here.

Chet was charged him with the crime of "transportation of a large sum of money," which was intended to be dropped at his court appearance in exchange for the cash. But Chet had done nothing wrong, and he wanted his money back. He needed it to take the real estate course and start a new career. So after his sister posted bond, they hired local El Paso attorney Luis Islas, who said he was a friend of the judge and could take care of the misunderstanding.

However, when they went to court, the agents and the prosecutor from the U.S. Attorney's Office were waiting for them outside the courthouse. The agents may not have known that having cash from provably legal sources like rodeos and welding jobs was not a crime. However, the prosecutor did, so when he learned that Chet had hired an attorney, he changed the charge to "possession of marijuana" and informed them of this change on the courthouse steps. This despite the fact that Chet had not possessed any marijuana—the only marijuana present at the entrapment setup was what the agents said they had in their possession and unsuccessfully attempted to sell to Chet. So Chet was charged for the illegal drugs that *they* had in their possession—assuming they were not lying about that too, as he never saw it.

The prosecutor had not been made aware of this fact, and when he found out, he knew he had a problem. So he changed the charges for a third time, supposedly before a grand jury (although the bill of indictment was not signed, rendering it worthless). At this point, even if it had been a real indictment, it was dated 110 days after the night of Chet's arrest, which made it void under federal law.[1]

The unsigned bill of indictment left the knowingly false charge of possession of (the government's) marijuana, which Chet had never even seen, but added "attempt to conspire to possess marijuana" to insure the win, as there is no defense against a charge of "conspiracy" (a subject we will explore in more depth later). The possession charge was left as a bargaining chip to try and get a plea deal from Chet and his attorney—if he pled guilty to the attempt to conspire charge, they would drop the (knowingly false) possession charge.

All the government had to do at this point was find a "co-conspirator" who would say that he or she knew Chester, and that he wanted to do a marijuana deal. Chet did not know anyone when he arrived, but there were plenty of time-cut artists there who were willing to trade false testimony for a reduction in their own sentences.

This third attempt to fabricate a crime occurred far beyond the 30 days allowed under the law to add a charge or change

---

1 18 U.S. Code § 3161(b) requires any additional charge to be added within 30 days from arrest or indictment.

those made after arrest (18 U.S.C. §3161(b)) and was highly illegal—not to mention that there is no law against "attempting to conspire to obtain marijuana." But again, that's just the law.

Judge Montalvo ordered Chet to go into a room, meet with the representatives from the U.S. Attorney's Office, and make a deal. He indicated that Chet would be set free after the meeting and could then "apply" to get his money back. When Chet walked in, however, the government attorneys and agents immediately began trying to get him to say that he knew of some marijuana deal and would testify against others about it.

"But I don't know about anything about any marijuana deal," he told them. The agents assured Chet that this was not a problem. All he had to do was *say* he knew of a deal. But Chet refused. In Fed-speak, that is known as "refusal to cooperate."

When the first tack failed, the agents asked Chet to give names of people he thought *might* be in the marijuana business, and agree to testify against them. "But I don't know anybody in that business. I rope steers and weld," he told them. The agents again assured Chet that this was not a problem. All he had to do was *say* he knew of a deal.

But Chet again refused to lie (a.k.a. "cooperate"). The agents and government attorneys kept pushing him. That's when the cowboy in Chet came out.

He said something along the lines of, "Well it may not be a *problem* for you sons of bitches, but it's a problem for me, because you're asking me to lie. I'm not going to lie to you, and I'm damn sure not going to lie for you. This meeting is over."

According to Chet, the agents and attorneys seemed shocked that they had run across a man who refused their "deal." It seemed to be a very new experience for them. Whether or not Judge Montalvo knew the essence of the conversation, he was told by the prosecutors that Chet had "refused to cooperate," so Judge Montalvo ordered Chet and his attorney into the courtroom.

The judge then claimed that they had made a "deal" and Chet had refused to keep his end of it. When Chet tried to tell the judge what the agents and prosecutors had suggested, his attorney told him to be quiet and said that he would "take care of it."

That's when Judge Montalvo decided to turn Chet's probable cause hearing into a sentencing hearing and remanded him to several years in federal prison, with consecutive sentences for the violation of laws that do not exist and crimes never committed, on charges which had been filed 80 days beyond the limit allowed under federal law.

Before Chet could object, appeal, or confront his attorney for misleading him as to what was happening, it was over. He was clapped in irons and sent to a prison in Texas, where they used his welding skills to turn Hummers into bulletproof vehicles for U.S. government officials and judges who need protection. Considering the system they operate under, there is little doubt as to why.

By the time I heard about Chester Ray Williams and his case, he had been moved all the way from Texas to a federal prison built on top of an old coal mine in Beaver, West Virginia. I suppose Judge Frank Montalvo wanted Chet as far away from El Paso as he could get him.

After reviewing the case, I filed an appeal for Chet, based on the substantial violations of his constitutional rights, including charges that were knowingly false, never proven, and did not exist under U.S. law, as well as the tardy changes and unsigned Bill of Indictment, which legally voided the whole matter. We also filed a judicial complaint with the Fifth Circuit Judicial Council against Judge Frank Montalvo for what he had done in the case. He was acting as a prosecutor rather than a judge, and violated Chet's rights, which needed to be on record. I had another motive for this filing—the fact that such complaints never, ever result in punishment of the judge.[2]

The case was remanded by the Fifth Circuit, to the same judge who had violated those rights and committed the crimes against Chet—the Honorable Frank Montalvo. He was tasked with determining whether he had done anything wrong or not. By filing the judicial complaint in New Orleans, however, we knew that the Circuit Court would be aware of what Judge Montalvo had done by the time our appeal reached them. I suppose Montalvo realized this as well, because he eventually ruled in our favor to avoid our inevitable appeal.

Judge Montalvo reluctantly admitted that he had sent this man to prison for a law that does not exist . . . that's the good news . . . but he waited until just *three days* before Chet was to be released from his unlawful sentence to do so. And that is still not the end of the story. Judge Montalvo took it upon himself to change the false charge of "possession of marijuana" to "attempt to possess marijuana," outside of any legal authority, years after the case had been adjudicated, and then refused to overturn his "new" charge, so Chet would still have a federal criminal record.

The fact that federal judges can break the law with such complete impunity and immunity, as well as lack of scrutiny (or penalty), is a very serious problem in America. This man acted as judge, grand jury, prosecutor, and petit jury, and then apparently tried playing God by going back in time and altering false charges made years before.

---

2 Attorney John Dean, former White House Council, did a study of 1,000 complaints of judicial crimes and misbehavior filed by attorneys with judicial councils around the nation (this is the only recourse one has against a judge . . . to file a complaint with his "peers") and wrongdoing, though often proven, was not found by them in a single case. No sanctions were issued. It should be clear by now that this system is no different from letting (other) criminals form panels and decide if they did anything wrong or not as well.

But that is still not all. As payback for our "win," Judge Montalvo ordered Chet to be carted all the way to Oklahoma City just three days before his release date, where he was held for a month beyond that date, and then taken to El Paso on a prison bus, in chains, for "re-sentencing." Only then was Chester Ray Williams released.

That, unfortunately, is as close as you can get to a "win" today in our system of American justice.

Chet's sister fought with the El Paso court and as far up the ladder as the attorney general of the United States for months. She fought until she got Chet's fine for the overturned charge released and the money government had stolen from him returned, so he could get his knee fixed and buy a truck. Still, he is now back to roping and rodeoing at age 63—because there is nothing else he can do with a big Scarlet "F" on his chest in the state of Texas.

But there may still be hope for that real estate career. I just heard from Chet, whom I now consider a dear friend, and the neighboring state of New Mexico is going to let him come there and get his license after all.

All I can say is that Texas's loss is New Mexico's gain.

CHAPTER 5

Restore Jury Rights

As originally designed by our nation's founders, trial by jury is one of the greatest protections an American citizen has from government overreach. The verdict of a jury is unreviewable, and a vote of not guilty from a single juror, for any reason, renders the accused not guilty and saves him or her from penalty. This gives each juror the power to rule not only on the facts of the case, but also on the law itself, and makes an informed juror more powerful than any judge, lawmaker, or even the president—none of whom have such leeway to rule on or void law.

This was a very important piece of our Founding Fathers' plan. The courts were considered the province of the people and were designed to be their ultimate protection against government power and abuse.

Unfortunately, this is no longer the case. The juror still has the same rights and powers, but is no longer advised of them, despite the fact that a thorough explanation of a jury's powers was once a traditional part of jury instructions in every court. Today's judges give juries the opposite information, as part of what seems to be a sad conspiracy between public prosecutors and judges (mostly former prosecutors themselves) to keep the conviction rate as high as possible.

Jury rights were also an important piece of the balance of power between government and the governed. Each individual juror had (and still has, according to the Constitution) the power to refuse to enforce bad laws. This is how We the People forced Congress to undo the Alien and Sedition Acts, the Fugitive Slave Act, and other harmful laws throughout our history. Jurors refused to convict their fellow citizens until Congress was forced to reexamine the laws, ultimately realizing their overreach and rescinding them (or in the case of the Alien and Sedition Acts, allowed them to expire).

This process is known as *jury nullification*, and it needs to become part of our judicial landscape once again as part of jury instructions in every state and federal court in the nation. It is still the law and our constitutional right when serving as jurors, but it cannot prevent abuse unless citizens know or are informed of their rights and powers.

Our founders intended for jurors to control the courts, rather than judges or prosecutors. They were quite clear on this issue. Both Alexander Hamilton[1] and John Adams[2] stated that it was the jury's power to rule on both the facts in a case and the law itself, a view that was encouraged at the time by the courts. The judge was little more than a referee and was not even required to have a law license in most states until the last century. In my home state of North Carolina, as example, this did not occur until lawyers took control of our legislature in 1979.

As recently as the 1970s, rulings such as *U.S. v. Dougherty* were still informing jurors of their unreviewable and un-reversible power "to acquit in disregard of the instructions on the law given by the trial judge" (473 F. 2nd, 1139 [1972]). As Supreme Court Chief Justice John Jay wrote in 1789, "The

---

1   "It is essential to the security and personal rights and public liberty, that the jury should have and exercise the power to judge both of the law and the criminal intent." Alexander Hamilton, founder, vice president of the United States, and trial attorney, in case 3 Johns, Cas 336 (1804).

2   "It is not only [the juror's] right, but his duty . . . to find the verdict according to his own best understanding, judgment, and conscience, though in direct opposition to the directions of the court." John Adams, 1771, founder and second president of the United States. *The Works of John Adams*, by C.F. Adams, pp. 253–255 (1856).

jury has the right to judge both the law as well as the fact in controversy."

However, a lawyer bringing up the subject of jury rights in a court at the state or federal level today would likely face sanctions. Public prosecutors currently run the courts at both the state and federal levels, and only the rare student of history who finds him or herself on a jury knows of these rights and powers going in.

As a teenager, I often drove my grandfather, who was a famous trial attorney, to court, and I frequently witnessed judges giving jury instructions. They would remind jurors of their right and power to rule on the facts of the case as well as the law itself. Jurors were told that for any reason, including their personal belief that the law was unfair or was in conflict with their beliefs or those of their community, they had the power to acquit the defendant.

While judges no longer notify juries of that power (and responsibility), prosecutors today are compounding the problem by no longer allowing juries to know or be advised of the punishment the defendant they judge is facing. I have interviewed many jurors who, after learning in the news that defendants they found guilty were sentenced to decades in prison, say they would never have found them guilty had they known the degree of punishment they were facing.

That's why judges and prosecutors no longer inform juries of the penalties associated with conviction. No reasonable person would sentence someone to decades in prison for marijuana, yet 47 percent of those in America's system of mass incarceration are there for that reason. Lengthy mandatory sentences for minor crimes have given the United States the dubious honor of handing out the harshest sentences, on average, of any nation on earth.

Congress has had a major hand in this misadventure. In 1996, the same year our elected representatives bound and shackled our rights of *habeas corpus* with A.E.D.P.A., they also created mandatory minimum sentences for many crimes. On top of this, they instituted "three strikes" laws sending a person to prison for life—even for a minor infraction like shoplifting—if it was their third offense.

If a jury was informed that a defendant would be going to prison *for life* for shoplifting, it is highly unlikely that that person would be found guilty. The time does not in any way match the crime. However, prosecutors and judges also know this, which is why they withhold this information from the juries they rely on to deliver a guilty verdict.

The injustices continue after the jury leaves the room, in the form of what are called "enhancements." Judges, the majority of whom are former public prosecutors, also control the probation departments that compile PSRs (pre-sentence reports). In a PSR, the defendant's entire life history can be taken into account, including any misconduct, even if the sentence for that misconduct has been served in full. At the same time, any good things the defendant has done are usually ignored. Enhancements of months or even years are then added to the defendant's sentence based on this previous conduct, even though that conduct had nothing to do with the crime for which they are being punished.

To remedy this situation, we should require these sentencing proposals to be submitted to the jury so in every case, they can then make an informed decision about finding the defendant guilty or not. If the punishment is ridiculous, any jury member can save the jury (and the taxpayer) from making a grave error by setting the defendant free with a single vote against conviction.

Currently, our system is designed to over-punish at every turn, using tools provided by legislatures which often exceed the authority granted to those bodies by the citizens. It has been further perverted by public prosecutors and judges who act without any restraint or meaningful oversight. They have collectively brought us to this state. We must return control of our courts to our juries if the national disgrace of mass incarceration is ever to be seriously addressed.

ACTION ITEMS FOR RESTORING JURY RIGHTS

1. Jury instructions given by judges in every criminal case, whether state or federal, must include a full explanation of jurors' rights.
2. All courts must submit the maximum sentence being sought by both the prosecutor *and* the judge's probation officers to the jury *before* their deliberations on guilt or innocence begin so they know the penalty that may be applied if the person is found guilty.
3. Pre-sentence reports should be eliminated from the process altogether, or required to tell the full story of the defendant, including the good that they have done. These reports should be submitted to the jury as well.
4. Ultimately juries should determine sentences, not Congress, prosecutors, or judges.

The Todd Ashworth Story

Hamlin, West Virginia, once had a hero. Tall, lanky, smooth walking—the nicest guy you would ever want to meet. Everybody loved Todd Ashworth.

Handsome but humble, generous but a tough competitor, Todd scored big in everything he did, including on the basketball court. He was Hamlin's hero.

Todd married his sweetheart, Susan, and they had two sons, Jacob and Lucas. Life was good. The boys were growing up, and Todd's greatest pleasure was teaching them sports and spending time together as a family. But that came to an end one day.

When Todd was young, much like all of our presidents of the last 25 years, he experimented with drugs. He quit when he and Susan got serious and never did them again, to the point where he even refused to hang around with anyone who used drugs. After all, he had a wife and two boys to think of.

However, despite the fact that Todd had not had any interest in drugs for years, an old school acquaintance started coming by his house, asking where he could find drugs. We'll call him Guy #1. Todd's answer to Guy #1 was always the same: He would tell him he had no idea since he had not used drugs for years, and then he would ask him to leave. But Guy #1 kept coming back again and again, and each time, he acted more desperate.

One night, when Susan was away visiting her mother, Guy #1 came back yet again, and this time Todd reached his breaking point. He ordered him to stay away or he would call the police. At this point, Guy #1 proposed a deal. If Todd would just introduce him to anyone—anyone at all—who was still involved with drugs, he would leave Todd alone and never come back.

Keep in mind that this happened in West Virginia, the state *The Economist* reported led the nation in the abuse of pharmacological substances back in 2010. As of January 2016, there is still a major epidemic; for example, "The main pharmacy in Kermit, West Virginia—a town of 400—fills more prescriptions for oxycodone than all but 21 pharmacies in the U.S."[1] Oxycodone is so big in West Virginia these days that the locals are called "pill-billies" rather than hillbillies. Which means that everyone—including Todd—knows somebody who is involved with drugs.

So Todd agreed to introduce Guy #1 to a guy that everybody in town knew sold drugs. We'll call him Guy #2. Guy #1 promised that, in exchange, he would never set foot on Todd's property again.

Todd introduced Guy #1 to Guy #2: "Hey, I knew this guy in school and he's looking to make some friends. I'm outta here." No drugs were seen or exchanged in Todd's presence. He went home and never saw Guy #1 again . . .

. . . until he was indicted as Guy #2's "coconspirator" in an alleged drug distribution scheme, arrested, and thrown in jail.

Todd knew he had committed no crime, so he hired a lawyer and went to trial. This was problematic for the U.S. Attorney's Office—if Todd was not found guilty, it could blow their case against Guy #2. Guy #1—Todd's persistent acquaintance— was actually working for the government as an *agent*, someone who by law cannot be listed as a "conspirator." Guy #1 was attempting to make cases against anybody he could in exchange for not going to prison for his own activities as a drug dealer.

---

1 CBS *Evening News* with Scott Pelley, January 8, 2016.

If they could not get Todd to plead guilty, they would lose the case against Guy #2.

Threats did not work on Todd, and he went to trial. And even though he was acquitted by a jury on the charge of "conspiracy," the U.S. Attorney's Office in the Southern District of West Virginia put him in prison for 10 years anyway, to protect the conviction of Guy #2—Todd's alleged "coconspirator."

Remember, the decisions of a jury are unreviewable. They cannot be challenged for any reason, and once a defendant is *acquitted*, that term means that there can be no punishment of the defendant, period, for that charge. It's supposed to be over. But it wasn't over for Todd.

When I began working on Todd's case in 2010, I was appalled to learn that the U.S. Attorney's Office had been successful in getting the Fourth Circuit Court of Appeals to condone their unlawful actions and Todd's resulting false imprisonment on charges acquitted by a jury. The Fourth Circuit has the reputation among those of us who work in this arena as a particularly bad actor when it comes to rubber-stamping wrongs committed by the government. And Todd Ashworth—father, husband, and local hero—spent 10 years in federal prison for a charge that he was acquitted of by a jury of his peers, in violation of everything for which our nation's judicial system once stood. Like so many people who lose their freedom in this manner, he lost his wife and became estranged from his sons. When he was released from prison after 10 years, he had nothing to which to return.

We filed an appeal to the court in West Virginia that had allowed the error, but the case was dismissed by Federal Judge Irene C. Berger without ever addressing the issue—that a jury had acquitted the charge. We then appealed to the Fourth Circuit, despite their history of failure to right this wrong, and they also dismissed the case without addressing either this issue or their own previous error in allowing the punishment to stand. We continued to fight, taking the case all the way to the United

States Supreme Court, but the appeal was denied *certiorari*, meaning that The Supreme Court of the United States would not even give Todd a hearing.

Cases like Todd Ashworth's have emboldened U.S. Attorney's Offices and prosecutors alike to become serial lawbreakers themselves. They know from the top that the likelihood of their crimes ever being officially acknowledged is even lower than the odds of one of their victims getting justice in their courts. The fact that government can simply ignore a jury's verdict without consequence means that today's juries are just for show. Restoring the jury's constitutionally mandated power to We the People is necessary if we are ever going to reform this broken system.

CHAPTER 6

Restore Parole

Until 1984, a citizen serving a lengthy prison sentence had every reason to try to achieve rehabilitation. If the citizen was determined not to be a threat to society and behaved well during incarceration, the law at the time allowed that person to be paroled *during* or *within* their sentence. Even in the case of lengthy sentences, a prisoner displaying good behavior and rehabilitation went home after a few years behind bars.

These prisoners were not completely on their own—they continued to be monitored within the time frame of their sentence, and if they proved themselves unready, they were returned to prison to complete that sentence there. But once that (original) sentence was completed, they were completely free. They had paid their debt to society.

This system worked well. Families were often able to survive a member's incarceration; something that rarely happens in light of today's lengthier sentences. Society benefited from the return of working, taxpaying citizens who contributed to their communities. Releasing prisoners who were not a danger to society saved taxpayers the tens of thousands of dollars each year it cost to keep a single prisoner incarcerated.

In 1984, after nearly a decade of debate, all of that changed.

The Omnibus Comprehensive Crime Control Act actually began in 1975, with the introduction of a bill by Senator Edward M. Kennedy authorizing judicial conference appointment of a commission for the purpose of promulgating sentencing guidelines for court consideration. Senator Kennedy saw this as "the beginning of a concerted legislative effort to deal with sentencing disparity."

The next three Congresses tried to comprehensively reform the federal criminal code to reduce disparity in sentencing. Eventually, they succeeded—but not in a good way. The Senate bill progressively tightened intended guideline constraints on judicial discretion and decreased the relative influence of the Judiciary over the construction of the guidelines (while increasing the role of the Executive Branch). This handed significant power to the political party controlling the White House, giving them an added tool to use against those in opposition.[1]

The end result of this decade of congressional tinkering was, in short, a disaster. Judges lost much of their historical discretion, and sentence disparity was reduced by making *everyone* do much more time in prison. The one-size-fits-all legislation did away with parole, and required every prisoner to serve a minimum of 85 percent of their sentence, filling every prison in the country to full and even overflowing— capacity is currently at 130 percent.

This was the beginning of the mass incarceration crisis and the prison-industrial complex in the United States. Today, without the possibility of parole, the incentive to behave well in prison is also gone. Gangs and gang memberships in prisons have exploded. Violence and sexual assault have escalated as well.

Judges have been reduced to mere robots, calculating predetermined sentences that allow little if any discretion or the consideration of individual circumstances and factors. The harsh sentences mandated for a preset range of minor crimes benefit no one except the prison-industrial complex. And the

---

1 University of Missouri Professor Donald C. Shields undertook pioneering research proving that the Bush Justice Department prosecuted Democrats at a 7:1 ratio in official corruption investigations during its first seven years (https://andrewkreig.wordpress.com/tag/political-prosecution/). Prosecutions of Republican and conservative groups by the Obama Administration is approximately the same in reverse: 7:1 Republicans to Democrats.

prison industry has become one of America's fastest growing businesses as a direct result of this misguided legislation.

With only 5 percent of the world's population, the United States now holds 25 percent of its prisoners. A citizen in "The Land of the Free"[2] is 32 times more likely to be in prison or on probation than a citizen of Communist China. No dictator, tyrant, or "evil empire"[3] has ever come close to what the last five presidents of the United States have done to their own people.

In addition to eliminating parole and extending the back end of sentences, another aspect of this so-called reform worked on the front end—by essentially eliminating bail for over three-quarters of all detainees. The Bail Reform Act allowed prosecutors to hold prisoners indefinitely by labeling them a "flight risk" or a "danger to the community." Suddenly, every defendant was both a flight risk *and* a danger to the community, (except those who were guilty and pled so, or were released, like Whitey Bulger, to work for the government on the streets). The only noticeable change that resulted from the Bail Reform Act was not any sort of "reform," but the destruction of the Constitutional right guaranteed in Amendment 8: to be free to prepare for trial. Locked in jail, many citizens are unable to secure effective counsel or gather witnesses. No wonder the conviction rate of American defendants has since climbed to the highest on earth—98.7 percent.

Restoring the right to bail so citizens are again able to prepare for trial will rapidly reduce the rate of plea bargains.

---

2 The term "Land of the Free" is from Francis Scott Key's song, "The Star-Spangled Banner," which was—oddly enough—written while he was being held prisoner on a warship in 1814.

3 President Ronald Reagan coined the term "evil empire" to refer to the Soviet Union and its prison gulags in a 1983 speech. The number of prisoners now held in America's gulags far exceeds that of the Soviet Union at any point in its history.

Similarly, by restoring parole, the system can begin to slowly correct itself at the other end of the sentence.

Good behavior once meant early release—a big carrot for someone serving 20 years in prison. And there is no attempt in federal prisons or (most) state prisons any longer to reha- bilitate prisoners, so these releases should be granted liberally. All the current system is doing is creating anti-social beings, most of whom will be released back into society one day any- way. According to a study released by Allen J. Beck of the Department of Justice, Bureau of Statistics, even a short stint in a county jail can increase the tendency of an otherwise non- criminal citizen to become one by threefold. So why put the nonviolent there in the first place? At is stands, the billions of taxpayer dollars saved by releasing nonviolent prisoners *within* their sentences could be used to educate and help those within the system to eventually rejoin society with a skill and a purpose.

Unfortunately, this is not the full extent of the damage wrought by the Bail Reform Act. In addition to essentially elim- inating bail and completely doing away with parole, Congress added a second sentence to almost every one handed down by the court, with what is called "supervised release".

The original legislation clearly indicates that the tool of supervised release was to be used sparingly—only for the most dangerous prisoners, or as assistance for those who had no one to help them when they were released. Instead, super- vised release is routinely included, for years or even life, as part of the punishment in nearly all sentences. In fact, I have never seen a case where the judge did not add this second sentence.

This has resulted in America also having the highest *recidivism* rate—the rate at which freed citizens are re-imprisoned—in the world. The Bureau of Justice Statistics released new informa- tion on recidivism rates among former prisoners in 2014—and while the numbers aren't surprising, they are disturbing.

The study, released Tuesday, tracked 404,638 state prisoners from 30 states who were released in 2005. It found that
67.8 percent of them were re-arrested within three years of
their release and 76.6 percent were re-arrested within five
years. Of the latter group, more than a third were re-arrested
in the first six months after leaving prison, and more than
half were arrested by the end of the first year, showing that
the rate of recidivism was highest during the first year and
declined every year after that.[4]

This was inevitable, as putting citizens under intense scrutiny
after their sentence is completed and making violations of rules
that are not even laws reason enough to return them to prison
seems like a foolproof plan to keep prisons full.

Most citizens fail in their first year out of prison, not necessarily due to criminal acts or intent, but because of the system
of supervised release itself. After the first year, a citizen can
apply to have supervised release ended, which is the real reason the rearrest rate drops in the study. During that first year,
however, with a parole officer constantly monitoring their
activities, entering their homes without warning, demanding
urine tests and a monthly report of all activities, the chances of
a released prisoner slipping up and being sent back to prison
are high—even though their actual sentence has already been
completed in full.

With 314,000 crimes to choose from, slipping up is easy, and
an entire private industry has appeared to profit from it—*the
halfway house* business. Private organizations and individuals take old buildings or motels and turn them into what are,
essentially, low security, privately run prisons for those on
"supervised release." The halfway houses determine their own,
very strict rules for living there, and also enforce those rules

---

4 Caitlin Dickson, "America's Recidivism Nightmare," *The Daily Beast*,
April 22, 2014; http://www.thedailybeast.com/articles/2014/04/22/america
-s-recidivism-nightmare.html.

and determine when a resident who has been ordered to stay at their facility is in violation. This occurs in two out of three cases, indicating a severe problem with this system.

Prison case managers, as they are called, give recommendations as to how many months a prisoner should stay in a halfway house, and there is strong evidence that they are well-compensated by private halfway house owners for making those stays lengthy. If six months is recommended by the case manager for the released prisoner to stay, the halfway house gets paid for six months, even if they release the prisoner on the day of arrival, which is completely within their discretion and happens quite often. And whether a stay ends up being a day or six months, privately run prisons are always paid in full. Just like in gambling, the house always wins. The halfway house gets to lease the same bed, again and again. As you might imagine, this is costing taxpayers a fortune.

I asked a CPA, who was released from prison in 2010, to keep records of what was being done in a halfway house in Charlotte, North Carolina. The halfway house was located in a former cheap motel where the rooms' doors had been removed and bunk beds installed, sleeping four men to a room. According to the CPA, at the turnover rate of release, each room was generating an average of $2,400 per day. That's a lot more lucrative than the old Motel Six was back when Tom Bodett promised to leave the light on for $29 a night.

Privately run halfway houses average $32,000 per year, per resident in lower cost areas like Charlotte, North Carolina, while the cost can be twice as high in places like New York. When the halfway house operators return two of every three residents to prison, they do so knowing that they will be cashing in again when the prisoner returns after their next release—and often again and again, as the story following this chapter confirms.

No wonder American prisons are now revolving doors: someone is making money at every turn. The system is designed to maximize occupancy at every level, even after the prisoner has served his or her sentence in full.

Instead of that, here's a radical idea. When the sentence is over, why not end punishment the way we once did? Supervised release serves no one but the prison industry and must be abolished.

ACTION ITEMS FOR RESTORING PAROLE

1. Bail is a constitutional right (Amendment 8), and it must be restored so that all citizens accused of a crime are free to prepare for trial.
2. Parole should be restored as a sensible means of reducing costs and ending the destructive social effects of harsh, unrelenting sentences from which there is no possible relief.
3. Supervised release is a potentially unending second sentence after the prisoner has served his or her sentence in full, amounting to punishing the citizen twice (or more) for the same crime. Supervised release must end except in the case of (documented) extraordinarily violent citizens.

The Randolph Wilson Story

Supervised release is almost always unlawful, unconstitutional, and immoral. However, it has also been added to every case I have studied or reviewed. Therefore, the story of Randolph Wilson can apply to any person in America who might be leaving prison—which is something that every taxpayer *and* human rights activist should be aware of.

Randolph Wilson (or "R. Dub," as everyone who knows him calls him) could be a double for Alfred E. Newman, the character on the front of *MAD* magazine. He has freckles, a broad face and smile and seems eternally youthful, despite the fact that he recently turned 35.

Back in 2010, District Court Judge John T. Conpenhaver of the Southern District of West Virginia sent Randolph back to prison for alleged violations of his supervised release at Transitions, Inc., a privately owned halfway house in Kentucky. This alleged violation occurred after Randolph's sentence for teenage drug use was served in full—something that happens every day in every court in the United States of America. For Randolph, it was the beginning of a seemingly endless cycle.

Over and over again, Randolph was returned to prison for alleged "violations" of privately run halfway house rules during the additional sentence imposed by supervised release. He wound up spending more time in jails and prisons *after* his sentence was completed in full, making his "additional sentence" longer than his original sentence. This essentially amounts to being punished twice for the same crime, with one of those punishments in potential perpetuity—something for which there is no justification under the United States Constitution.

Randolph has now spent his entire youth in federal prisons and private halfway houses. He has no skills, no training, and very little hope of getting any, all because he used drugs as a teenager. Admittedly, there is nothing newsworthy in the story of a guy being sent back to prison, as we already know it happens to 76.6 percent of Americans who have served their time in full. What makes Randolph's story stand out from those of his fellow recidivists is that this was the fifth time.

Randolph was sent back to prison five times—*after* paying his debt to society in full—for violations of "rules" (not laws) that were established by the halfway house. Ironically (or not), those rules ensure that halfway houses receive a steady stream of residents and every prison is kept full.[1] It's an endless revolving door, and a lucrative one.

During one stint, the halfway house sent Randolph home to live before the recommended time was up, even though they were paid in full to keep him there and support him. They were then free to sell the bed again, while still collecting all of the money for Randolph's six-month stay, which was roughly $32,000, plus a quarter of his earnings.

Then they turned him in—for the horrific crime of writing a letter to friend. So Randolph could reenter prison and later, return to the halfway house through the revolving door again. And the halfway house could be paid approximately $32,000 from the U.S. government, plus 25 percent of everything Randolph earned, again and again, every time they sent him back.

What was formerly a Motel Six now brings in $72,000 (or more) a month *for each room*, plus 25 percent of each

---

1 "According to the study, [concerning prison overcrowding] federal prisons were 39% over capacity as of September 2011. Further, the report predicted that overcrowding would climb to more than 45% above the BOP's maximum capacity by 2018"; https://www.prisonlegalnews.org/news/2014/may/19/report-increase-federal-prison-population-overcrowding/.

guests' paycheck (before taxes and deductions), during the entire period of supervision. And now these privately owned quasi-prisons have made it a rule that the *crime* of not being able to find a job is reason enough to send the citizen back to prison as well. These are not good odds for the citizen, since getting a job after being labeled a felon is almost impossible. This keeps the citizen, who has long since served his time for his crime, going around and around through the revolving door, while everybody else gets paid a second time, a third, a fourth, and in the case of Randolph Wilson, a fifth time, and maybe more. The case manager at the prison will get another gift each time he sends the halfway house more business— even if it is the same customer.[2] The halfway house will make another $32,000 or more, plus 25 percent of the freed citizen's paycheck for several months. The members of the prison guard union will have another few months of "job security."[3]

---

2 This is admittedly speculation, as neither case managers or their bosses would admit to me that they were being paid by Halfway Houses, but they also did not deny it. The exact quote from two of those interviewed was the same from both, "It's none of your fucking business." The anecdotal evidence is also strong. The case manager at Randolph Wilson's prison (FCI Beckley) with whom I met personally (Thomas Carter) drove an old wreck of a car when he first moved from being a guard to the position as case manager. Within less than a year, Case Manager Carter was driving a shiny new black Hummer, the nicest car in the parking lot, including the warden's. His boss who soon arrived after that meeting, Unit Manager Michael Snow, began refusing to let any prisoner leave FCI Beckley without going to a halfway house, though it was their right to choose. Unit Manager Snow soon bought a nice fishing boat. I learned of this through a judge in Virginia who reported that Unit Manager Snow was caught speeding and driving his new boat recklessly—while drunk—in out-of-state Virginia, where he used the boat (Philpott Lake) rather than in West Virginia.

3 In an interview with Randolph Wilson's counselor at FCI Beckley, former prison union boss John Grimes, he stated, "All these motherfuckers are to us is job security, and we'll do whatever it takes to keep them here as long as we can." Mr. Grimes and other FCI Beckley officials were soon thereafter exposed and sued for falsifying prisoner's files. Prisoners' monthly work reports from their supervisors were put in the master files as "poor" and "fair" rather than "good" which was on the originals, so the inmates would not be eligible for six months' home release as the law requires. This

This story is not told in the recidivism rate numbers, but it is a major contributing factor to them. The government sends the citizen to prison, often wrongfully or outside of law, then labels them a felon for life. When these freed citizens can't get work because they are convicted felons, the government and the private halfway houses send them back to prison to start the whole cycle over again.

The private halfway houses have earned $160,000 so far, plus 25 percent of his earnings, by returning Randolph to prison again and again. His latest crime is—no joke—the aforementioned letter to a prisoner. The court opinion lists as its number one and number two reasons for returning him to prison: "1) That the defendant associated with a person convicted of a felony without the permission of the probation officer inasmuch on or about October 11, 2010, he sent a letter to a convicted felon incarcerated at FCI Beckley; 2) that the defendant failed to spend six months in a community confinement center as directed by the court inasmuch as he enrolled at Transitions, Inc. on August 10, 2010, and was terminated from the program on October 14, 2010, for failing to follow the rules and regulations at the facility by sending a written communication through the mail to an inmate incarcerated at FCI Beckley in which he admitted using illegal substances as defined by the Commonwealth of Kentucky criminal code."

The letter was a joke Randolph wrote to his best friend back in prison reporting that he was "sitting around the halfway house smoking salvia." The substance referred to, *salvia divinorum,* was still legal and not an illegal substance as the court, government, and halfway house falsely claimed, nor had

---

criminal conspiracy was reported to the Department of Justice as well as to the Bureau of Prisons and Federal District Court of Judge Irene C. Berger by suit, but no action was taken by either agency against the former union boss or those involved with him in the scheme, though the evidence (of which is still on file) was clear and overwhelming. Judge Berger dismissed the suit without a hearing.

Randolph done it. The "paraphernalia" they claimed to find when they searched his house was actually evidence from his original conviction for drug use many years before. They just recycled the evidence like they recycle Randolph in and out of prison. And you, the taxpayer, paid another $32,000 plus to the halfway house, as well as another small fortune to put Randolph Wilson back in federal prison, just because he sent a letter to another "felon." With 25 percent of the country now having a record, that rule would be hard for anyone not to break.

The worst part of the story, however, is the incredible hypocrisy of our government officials. While I was working on Randolph's supervised release violations, evidence of a criminal conspiracy by government employees to falsify official government files for an improper purpose was concurrently gathered and filed with the local U.S. District Court, Department of Justice, and Bureau of Prisons. The crime exposed cost the taxpayers an estimated $24 million dollars, yet as far as I can discern, it is still ongoing—because no one did anything about it. No government agency ever contacted me for an interview or full copies of the records. In fact, they ignored the entire matter. Nobody would do anything about this *real* crime involving government employees. Meanwhile, the District Court, U.S. Marshals Office, U.S. Probation Office, the Bureau of Prisons, and the private prison owners who profited from the scheme had plenty of time and considerable resources to dedicate to returning Randolph Wilson, teenage drug user, back to prison for the fifth time after he had completed his sentence in full.

The system is upside down. Real crimes committed by government officials are ignored and real criminals are sent back to the streets, while the innocent go to prison and are returned there time and again, simply to feed the prison-industrial complex and your representatives' campaign coffers.

This must stop.

CHAPTER 7

Eliminate Conspiracy Prosecutions

In the 1980s, federal law enforcement launched a massive push to take down the leaders of America's most powerful organized crime "families." Frustrated at these dangerous criminals' ability to avoid indictment, the government needed a means of bypassing due process of law in order to finally put these gangsters behind bars. So they re-designed and created a body of law known as "conspiracy."

"The essence of conspiracy," according to author Charles Doyle, "is an agreement of two or more persons to engage in some form of prohibited misconduct. Once they agree, the crime has been committed, although some statutes require prosecutors to show that at least one of the conspirators has taken some concrete step or committed some overt act in furtherance of the scheme."[1]

There are now dozens of federal conspiracy statutes, and most are problematic. One, 18 U.S.C. 371, outlaws any conspiracy to commit some other federal crime—and the sentence for the "conspiracy" is often greater than a citizen would have received if they were found guilty of the actual crime they were allegedly conspiring to commit. Worse, since Doyle wrote the definition above, there are now few laws that still require any overt act to make someone a "conspirator."

---

1 Charles Doyle, "Federal Conspiracy Law: A Brief Overview," April 30, 2010; Criminal Law Library blog; http://www.criminallawlibraryblog .com/2010/05/federal_conspiracy_law_a_sketc_1.html.

Throughout history, civilized nations have shunned anti-conspiracy laws. The ability for the government to abuse them is unlimited, making them among the most dangerous laws in our nation. This is also why the United States must abandon them.

When they first created them in the '80s, the Department of Justice argued that conspiracy laws were needed to enable them to get mob bosses like New York mafia don John Gotti and Cleveland gangster John "Peanuts" Trovolone off the streets. DOJ supposedly promised President Reagan and Congress that these new laws would only be used as a last resort in mob cases, and by this false promise, they were successful in getting them approved.

However, today these same conspiracy laws are used against ordinary citizens in an outrageous number of cases—nine of every ten on which I have worked. And, as in so many other cases I've reviewed over the years, the government always wins. Why? There simply is no defense against a charge that someone *thought* of committing a crime.

That's the beauty of conspiracy laws—and why the feds created them in the first place. They were unable to catch the mob bosses committing any crimes, but conspiracy laws gave them new crimes with which to charge them that required no evidence. Once the laws were in place, prosecutors simply worked their way up the ladder, starting by arresting the organized crime underlings who did most of the dirty work and offering them immunity or leniency (remember plea bargaining?) in exchange for their testimony. And all they had to say was that the boss *knew* of a criminal act.

The way conspiracy laws work, alleged conspirators may be punished for the conspiracy itself, as well as any completed substantive offense which is the object of the plot, plus any foreseeable offenses one of the other alleged conspirators commits in furtherance of the scheme. Since conspiracy is an omnipresent crime, it may be prosecuted wherever an overt act is committed in its furtherance, or without any overt act at all. Because it is a "continuing crime," the statute of limitations on conspiracy does not begin to run until the last alleged overt act has been committed for its benefit. However, a 2005 Supreme Court decision written by Sandra Day O'Connor states that no "overt act" is required at all, which would seemingly remove limitations of any kind.

Conspiracy is also a separate crime, so it may be prosecuted following conviction for the underlying substantive offense without violating constitutional double jeopardy principles. The courts have also ruled that it may be punished when it straddles enactment of the prohibiting statute without offending constitutional *ex post facto* principles. Accused conspirators are generally indicted and tried together, and any statement a prosecutor can coerce out of one of them may be admitted in evidence against all of them, making false testimony the hallmark of conspiracy prosecutions.

Clearly, this body of law is dangerous and problematic. An individual either commits a crime, or he or she does not. Conspiracy is merely a crime of thought. But the standard of regarding the mere thought of committing a crime or talking about it with another person as a crime in and of itself is too vague, and too easily abused in the hands of government—as time has proven.

Today, prosecutors frequently add a charge of alleged conspiracy as a safety net. If they're unable to prove that a crime was committed (or get their target to "voluntarily" admit to one), conspiracy laws make it possible to send the defendant to prison by claiming that he or she *thought* of committing a crime. Pages and pages of various "overt acts in furtherance of the conspiracy" are often added to indictments, not only providing an easier charge to prove should there be a trial, but also providing the added benefit of overwhelming jurors with too much information. When I asked one federal jury foreman if he or his fellow jurors ever read an entire indictment, his response was, "Hell no! They're too damn long! We just figured if it was that thick, somebody must of done something so we signed the bill of indictment."

Once an alleged conspiracy has been rubber-stamped by the grand jury, all of the alleged conspirators are arrested and jailed. In 77.1 percent of these cases, according to Department of Justice Bureau of Statistics director Allen J. Beck, they will be denied bond. Within days, the prosecutor will begin meeting with them, one by one, offering a deal to whomever agrees to talk about the others first. All the defendant has to do is say that he or she *conspired* with one or more of the other defendants—whether this is true or not—to get the deal. The prosecutor will make it clear that the others are being offered the same deal, and the last defendant to take it will likely be charged as the leader of the conspiracy and receive a much longer sentence.

If a defendant claims to be innocent, it makes no difference. Again, prosecutors are more focused on getting a conviction than in justice being served. Or, as onetime Assistant U.S. Attorney Matthew Martens explained to me when I interviewed him in 2006, the prevailing view, and the way DOJ trains its prosecutors, is "We believe all of you out there have done *something*. We just haven't gotten around to you yet."

Another common method of prosecution is the "jailhouse snitch" scenario, which is common in jails across America. Here, prosecutors encourage people who are in jail with the individual they are targeting to get close to that person and learn about their family, their likes and their dislikes so that they can credibly testify that they were friends. The snitch (or snitches, as the prosecutor usually employs two of them) then claims that the target admitted to considering a criminal act or to committing one. As a reward, the snitches' sentences are cut. At the same time, police or agents move in on the target's family members, associates, friends (and enemies), not-so-subtly threatening that they might be arrested and dragged into the case as well unless they agree to make a statement that the target was *thinking* of committing a crime.

For a citizen to be found guilty of conspiracy, two people must make that claim. This is why prosecutors usually employ two jailhouse snitches. However, if no coconspirator can be produced by the prosecutor, many will simply write "coconspirators, known and unknown" on the indictment, and this is usually enough for the grand jury to rubber stamp the case. The likelihood of a prosecutor ever having to prove that there really was a conspiracy is one in twenty, because, as we've already seen, 95 percent of their targets will plead guilty before a trial ever occurs. However, when necessary, prosecutors can usually come up with the two "witnesses" required through compensating and/or threatening others, whether those others know the target or not.

It's hard to imagine a more staggering level of injustice. Citizens now lie for government, against their fellow citizens, to save themselves—a practice for which we once condemned the Soviet Union. And despite the fact that the testimony of jailhouse informants and snitches is known to be unreliable, prosecutors continue to use them, creating convictions that could never have been honestly garnered.

Many European nations have stopped using testimony from co-defendants or granting them concessions due to the clear incentive to be less than truthful in exchange for leniency. If we are going to end our mass incarceration epidemic, the United States must follow their lead and restore truth and fairness to our judicial process.

ACTION ITEMS FOR
ELIMINATING CONSPIRACY PROSECUTIONS

---

1. Legislatively ban laws making a crime of thought illegal.

2. Repeal all conspiracy laws currently in effect except those regarding a plot to murder.
3. Legislatively eliminate the use of testimony of codefendants in alleged conspiracies to be used by prosecutors unless the case goes to trial.

The Dr. Edward Picardi Story

My name is Dr. Edward S.J. Picardi. I am a board-certified general surgeon (MD, F.A.C.S.), the former president of the South Dakota Chapter of the American College of Surgeons and a US Air Force veteran, husband, and philanthropist. I am also now a federal prisoner.

Why? Well, I'm still trying to sort that out myself, as I am in prison as a "sole" conspirator—an impossible crime—because I refused to give false testimony against someone else. I say "impossible crime" because the statute itself begins with the legal definition of conspiracy, stating, "If two or more persons conspire to commit any offense . . ."

There was no crime committed, so the government employed today's fallback catchall of "conspiracy," like they once charged people with mail fraud when they could not find a real crime. Their only mistake was forgetting to pair me with the "coconspirator" necessary to meet the definition of conspiracy. Of course, that doesn't seem to matter either, as there does not seem to be any legal oversight of what our prosecutors and judges are doing in the public's name, and no one to punish them for doing it.

My practice is now in shambles, my medical credentials have been revoked—though this nonsense had nothing to do with the practice of medicine—and it is quite possible that everything my wife, Sandy, and I worked for all of our lives will be gone when this nightmare ends.

BACKGROUND: I still remember the day it happened. Sandy and I were getting into the car after a day of treating patients, when four black Suburbans pulled up and blocked us. A number of individuals wearing bulletproof vests rushed out—an IRS agent who had come to my office some months before to ask me to testify against others among them. That agent rushed at me, telling me I was under arrest.

Five years earlier, I was visited at my home by two IRS agents. They told me the IRS wanted me to testify against an accountant/attorney I had worked with on one occasion in the past. One of the agents then told me that if I agreed to testify for them, the IRS would not come after me.

After me? For what? Everything I did was legal, and I paid good money to legal and financial professionals to make sure of it, but they still threatened me. It was intimated that they would find "something" to hurt me with if I did not play ball and do what they said.

The Assistant U.S. Attorney later confirmed to my attorney that if I testified for the IRS against the accountant/attorney at his upcoming trial, no federal felony charges would be filed against me. I would have to plead guilty to a single misdemeanor charge and pay a fine (I suppose to make the process look legal for the jury), but there would be no trial or risk of my losing my medical license. Hundreds of thousands of dollars could be saved in attorney's fees and I could go on living my life in peace without losing my medical license (which is automatic in South Dakota after a felony conviction). All I had to do was testify for the IRS against the accountant/attorney.

I seriously considered the "deal," as they kept calling it, until I learned what they wanted me to say. I asked the agent, point blank, "Do you want me to lie for you?" There was a slight pause.

Then the agent spoke the words that are forever embedded in my mind: "You're a smart guy. You know what this is about."

I replied that I had done nothing wrong to bargain about, so I would not accept any "offer" which required me to lie for the IRS.

The agent left his card on my desk, assuming I would change my mind, and I immediately hired a defense attorney, who contacted the agents involved with the case against the accountant/attorney to find out what was going on. When she reported back to me, she described the agents' attitude as "desperate." The attorney/accountant refused to plead guilty to something he had not done, and since they had nothing, they needed someone to help them fabricate a crime.

They were so desperate that the Assistant U.S. Attorney's office followed up with my attorney, calling her to remind her that no felony charges would be filed against me if I would just agree to testify against the accountant/attorney at his upcoming trial, and say what they told me to say.

So the lawyer/accountant the IRS had targeted refused to roll over and plead guilty like so many of their targets, leaving them, unexpectedly, with no case against him. No crime had been committed and all regulations and guidelines from the IRS had been followed, but the IRS charged him anyway, assuming he would plead guilty to avoid a harsher outcome at trial.

Whether he had broken a law or not did not seem to matter. They simply wanted to win against him, I suspect, so that they could seize the assets of his clients, some of which were quite substantial. If they could get the accountant/lawyer to say that he had broken the law, they could then get "voluntary" confessions and huge fines from his clients by using the same tactics to threaten them. Then they would cut a deal with the attorney/accountant to agree to testify against his clients in exchange for a cut in his sentence, and so on . . .

But it did not work out that way. And now, they wanted to use me to win their case for them. They wanted me to walk into a courtroom and say, "Yes, I committed a crime. I knowingly tried to avoid paying taxes on this attorney/accountant's advice." Because if I testified that I had knowingly done something wrong, by default, that meant the accountant/attorney must also have committed a crime as my professional advisor. He would have most likely been found guilty, the IRS would have won their case, and their target would have gone to jail.

As for me, I was simply a pawn to help the IRS get what they wanted, which was to win at all costs. The destruction of innocent lives, loss of careers, protecting everything that our Founding Fathers considered important in the framing of our nation had no relevance. The value of my life, the accountant/attorney's life and our families was nothing.

I soon learned that this is the hallmark of federal prosecutions today—they are designed so that the government wins, no matter what. That's how promotions are made, and how careers are advanced.

The 2004 book *Confessions of a Tax Collector: One Man's Tour of Duty Inside the IRS*[1] reveals this in great detail. The book explains exactly how agents are taught to break the law using "conspiracy" as their primary tool, pitting one citizen against another until one agrees to say that the other did something wrong.

And if they cannot find the required "coconspirator" to make the charge semi-legal, they can still send you to prison. Because that's what happened to me—I was sent to prison as a "sole" conspirator. My life has been destroyed, all so a couple of IRS agents can get promoted, or maybe just keep their jobs.

I am sharing my story in the hopes that I can help stop this from happening to anyone else.

---

1 Richard Yancey, *Confessions of a Tax Collector: One Man's Tour of Duty Inside the IRS* (New York: Harper Perennial, 2004).

CHAPTER 8

End Government Immunity

Why are judges and prosecutors not held accountable for their actions—even if they are criminal in nature? Through a string of court decisions beginning with *Pierson v. Ray* in 1967, our nation's judges and prosecutors have judicially granted themselves the status of being above the law. Even when they violate criminal statutes, as long as they are at work when they commit the crime, they are subject only to "peer review." This seems to be a clear violation of Amendment 14, and has given these public servants of bench and bar complete immunity for the crimes they commit against defendants.

As previously referenced, at a House Judiciary Committee hearing,[1] former White House Counsel, Attorney John Dean quoted that "More than 1000 formal complaints were filed against federal judges nationwide [in just one year]. The chief judges decided that not one of these cases required official discipline." In addition, "[i]n more than 450 cases, complainants appealed the dismissal of their complaint to the judicial council of an appellate court. These councils rejected every appeal."

According to this study, peer review results in an a 0 percent punishment rate for criminal acts by judges in these cases. We've already determined that those same judges' courts find 98.7 percent of those who come before them guilty. There is an interesting disparity between the way our judges judge

---

1 John W. Dean, Thoughts on the Law Addressing Bad *Federal Judges: Self-Policing Isn't Working, But Is There a Good Alternative?*; Aug. 13, 2004; http://writ.news.findlaw.com/dean/20040813.html.

themselves and the way they judge others. However, the daily crimes committed by judges are still in violation of federal law, and self-granted immunity by fiat and court decisions should not shield them from penalty of law.

18 U.S.C. §§ 241 & 242 make no exception for judges or any other government official who violates the rights of this nation's citizens. Section 242 states: "Whoever, under color of any law, statute, ordinance, regulation, or custom, willfully subjects any person in any State, Territory, Commonwealth, Possession, or District to the deprivation of any rights, privileges, or immunities secured or protected by the Constitution or laws of the United States . . . shall be fined or imprisoned . . . or both."

"Whoever" includes judges and prosecutors, as there are no stated exceptions.

Section 241 makes a conspiracy to deny a citizen's rights a criminal act. However, I've found conspiracies between prosecutors, attorneys, agents, and even judges in almost every case I've studied. A common example is the refusal of judges to try citizens within 70 days or to release them in 90 days, ignoring a federal criminal statute against such a violation. Frequently, they collude with prosecutors to hold citizens beyond that time period because they face no penalty for violations. But if Section 241 were enforced, these judges and prosecutors would spend 15 years in prison, in addition to one year for each violation of Section 242.

According to *Pierson v. Ray* and subsequent cases focusing on judicial (and prosecutorial) immunity, the reason usually given for the refusal to prosecute those involved in court decisions is to protect public figures from concerns about being sued while performing their pubic duties. But what about doctors, lawyers, and the rest of us? Professionals in other fields are routinely sued, frequently for mistakes that are far less harmful than wrongfully imprisoning a citizen, let alone executing one. Besides, the law requires "equal protection"—so does that mean that all should be exempt for their mistakes, or none? Legally, it has to be either one or the other. I submit that as public officials who swore an oath to uphold the U.S. Constitution, judges and prosecutors should suffer like anyone else when they knowingly violate it.

As it stands, the harm that these judges and prosecutors have been free to create is immense. In the case of that 73 percent of death-penalty defendants wrongfully put to death or sentenced to death row according to the Columbia Law School study, that harm is irreparable. A 73 percent failure rate is not merely unacceptable in any profession; it also serves as further evidence that self-granted immunity is a very bad idea which needs to be ended now. Making judges subject to law just like everyone else will force them to do a better job than they are currently doing under conditions of immunity.

Unfortunately, this will be a very difficult issue to tackle, because these same people decide what laws are enforced and who is prosecuted. There is an answer, however, and it begins with the simple act of raising awareness that this is a problem, and that it is serious. If research has proven that the majority of court decisions are tainted and full of errors, that indicates that judges, for the most part, are clearly not following the law and the Constitution. If they are subjected to penalty for error, or are forced to let a defendant go free when a violation is proven, the error rate would likely drop—precipitously, in my opinion.

It is understandable that judges need some protection during the performance of their public duty. However, the practice of allowing them to escape any and all penalty for knowing lawlessness is clearly not working. Congress is still empowered to remove bad federal judges, but that body rarely acts to impeach or remove anyone. Thomas Jefferson referred to judicial impeachment as "a mere scarecrow" back in 1826, and he appears to have been right.

So in the absence of help from Congress, judicial immunity should be severely limited or removed, making these public officials subject to penalty for illegal acts against the defendants who come before their courts. Petty grievances or bad decisions should be exempt, but any case where a judge clearly and knowingly violates the constitutional rights or statutory protections of a citizen should be prosecutable. If we want better, fairer, and more accurate results from our courts, then those who run them must face a real possibility of suffering penalty for violating the rights of those whose lives and livelihoods are in their hands. If these judges and prosecutors are unable or unwilling to act within the laws they swear to uphold, then perhaps they should find other work.

Another area that is desperately in need of reform is the Supreme Court of the United States. The body responsible for upholding the constitutional rights and protections of We the People has a terrible record of doing so. The Court enabled the conditions that led to the situation our nation is in today, and in many cases, it suborned them.

There is no requirement in the Constitution that Supreme Court justices must be attorneys—for good reason. James Madison, the man chiefly responsible for crafting the document, was not a lawyer, so it certainly should not take one to interpret his words. In fact, attorneys have shown a unique talent for misinterpreting the Constitution, and nine of them together in one court appear to ignore it altogether, finding words that are not there and refusing to acknowledge some that are.

As a solution, presidents can and should let some light and air into the institution by appointing non-lawyers to sit as justices. Constitutional scholars, historians, and those who have shown common sense in their work would be excellent candidates. Historically, some of our nation's best justices and Chief Justices have been self-trained or non-attorneys. Non-lawyers have been appointed to the Supreme Court as recently 1941, the last being James F. Byrnes, and one of the best known being Chief Justice John Marshall, who arguably had a greater influence on the direction of the Supreme Court than any before or since. Reviving the sound practice of including non-attorneys on the Court will bring common sense back to the bench, and may prompt it to again act on what the Constitution actually says.

A grand example of the lack of common sense plaguing our current Court is *Citizens United v. Federal Election Commission*, No. 08–205, 558 U.S. 310 (2010), a U.S. constitutional law case dealing with the regulation of campaign spending by corporations and other nonhuman entities. This 2010 decision is actually the culmination of 130 years of misinterpretation by that same Court, ostensibly beginning with an offhand comment that was made by a Supreme Court justice in 1886 before the case was even heard, but was left on the record. Since then, corporations have filed case upon case, piling one bad decision on top of the last in what is known as *stare decisis*.[2] The U.S. Supreme Court has now granted these nonhuman entities rights as "citizens," basically removing all limits on corporate political spending.

How does a box of papers and a seal become a "citizen," you and many others might ask? Good question, and one our current Supreme Court has shown complete ineptitude in answering, as the word "corporation" never appears a single time in the United States Constitution. This is not because our founders did not know of corporations, or "joint stock companies," as they were more commonly called back then. They knew of them and many of our founders despised them, Alexander Hamilton being a notable exception.

---

2   Stare decisis is a legal concept by which courts rely on the decisions of previous courts—even bad ones—to stand as basis for more recent decisions, but the Supreme Court did not actually rule on this issue, as has been claimed. "*Santa Clara County v. Southern Pacific Railroad Company*, 118 US 394 (1886) was a matter brought before the United States Supreme Court which dealt with taxation of railroad properties. A headnote issued by the Court Reporter claimed to state the sense of the Court regarding the equal protection clause of the Fourteenth Amendment as it applies to corporations, without the Court having actually made a decision or issued a written opinion on that issue." https://en.wikipedia.org/wiki/Santa_Clara_County _v._Southern_Pacific_Railroad_Co.

Thomas Jefferson said of these nonhuman entities, "I hope we shall crush in its birth the aristocracy of our monied corporations which dare already to challenge our government to a trial by strength, and bid defiance to the laws of our country." Those hardly sound like the words of a man who would consider granting these nonhuman entities the rights of American citizenship. So how did the United States Supreme Court reach the opposite conclusion?

Before Supreme Court tinkering began on this constitutionally absurd idea of corporate citizenship, it was a crime for a corporation to give money to a candidate. It was rightly called a bribe, and both the giver and the recipient could go to jail for it. Do our Chief Justice and his colleagues who supported the decision really believe that Jefferson and the others really intended for corporations to be "citizens," but forgot to put it in the Constitution? Or is even our highest court now for sale, as Congress has obviously been for decades thanks to this same string of obtuse Supreme Court decisions?

Adam Smith, the man known as the Father of Capitalism, held corporations in such low regard when he wrote *Wealth of Nations* in 1776 that he described them as "nuisances in every respect" that "have in the long run proved, universally, either burdensome or useless, and have either mismanaged or confined the trade."[3] Now those corporate entities enjoy the rights of citizenship, and thanks to the most recent actions of the U.S. Supreme Court, have the unlimited ability to buy any election.

When it comes to our Constitution, an historian or constitutional scholar is trained to study what was actually written. Attorneys, on the other hand, are trained to "interpret." This failure by the United States Supreme Court to follow the simple wording of our nation's contract between government and the

---

3 Smith, Adam. An Inquiry into the Nature and Causes *of the Wealth of Nations, Vol. 36, Chronology of Great Authors* (Chicago: Encyclopaedia Britannica, Inc. Sixth Edition, 1996), p. 313.

governed is little short of treason in the case of selling out our country to the highest corporate bidders. There is not much that can be done now to correct that—short of nine funerals—but future appointments to the Court must include persons trained to read the simple words of a non-attorney, Mr. James Madison, rather than "interpret" them.

As for the judges and prosecutors who seem complacent to live above the law, they need to be reminded of the real laws they swore to uphold in the Constitution, and must no longer be allowed to grant themselves privileges and protections not found in said document, or interpret words not found there for their own benefit or protection.

ACTION ITEMS FOR
ENDING GOVERNMENT IMMUNITY

1. Legislatively void any immunities or protections granted to prosecutors and judges by court decisions that give them a status different from those they were chosen to serve.
2. Encourage the appointment of non-attorneys to our court benches from the lowest to the highest, to restore common sense to decisions, rather than the following of bad precedents or "interpretation."
3. Legislatively void any court decision that acts to judicially add any powers or protections not specifically granted to the two parties of contact as stated in the United States Constitution (We the People and the United States Government).
4. Legislatively void any court decisions that act to judicially add parties, or to judicially rescind protections that were granted to either government or the People, in their contract—the Constitution of the United States.

The Michael Sherrill Story

Michael Sherrill had been accused of more murders than Jack the Ripper when I first met with him at Charlotte, North Carolina's infamous Mecklenburg County Jail back in 2006. He had already been held far beyond the legal time required for trial, while the local prosecutor, Peter Gilchrist, continued to try to force him to take a plea deal and admit to at least one murder. Because if he plead guilty to a killing, the local department could get millions in federal funding for solving what is known as a "cold case"—a case so old there is usually no one around to dispute what is claimed by the prosecutor.

However, Michael refused to admit to something he had not done. He is now on death row at Central Prison in Raleigh, North Carolina.

The longer Michael refused to plead guilty, the more cold cases the local prosecutor's office heaped on him, from other states all up and down America's East Coast. It is highly improbable that one man could be responsible for all of these crimes, and, in fact, Michael told me he could prove he was innocent. I asked him how.

"The trucking company I worked for used tracking," he explained. "They have records of every minute I was in that truck. I wasn't even in those places when these people were killed, but nobody will listen to me! Every time I tell them I'm innocent, they just throw on more cold case charges, trying to get me to take a plea."

Michael was correct. The trucking company's records proved beyond any doubt that out of the many additional charges brought against him (in an apparent attempt to get more federal money), all but two of the crimes occurred in places he could not have been. He was often hundreds or even thousands of miles away from where these crimes were committed. However, the prosecutor was not interested in the truth, no one checked the facts, and Michael's own attorney encouraged him to take the deal rather than go to trial.

District Attorney Gilchrist's zeal for coercing these plea deals was well-known and very much disliked, both by the victims of his wrongful prosecution, like Michael, and the families of the actual victims of real crimes. While he sent many of the citizens he accused who refused to plead guilty to death row, the victims' families accused Gilchrist of letting murderers off without adequate punishment. Once the D.A.'s office got a plea, in most cases, the real murderers went back to the streets in short order.[1]

Or, as the local Charlotte newspaper wrote after his retirement in 2010, "Gilchrist spent his years as district attorney enabling criminals with plea deals so outrageous that you could argue his prosecutors often victimized crime victims twice."[2]

Once the trucking company records were matched with the charges against Michael, District Attorney Gilchrist was forced to remove them. However, multiple capital charges were left from two cases back in 1984. Those two murders took place in Michael's home state, in the middle of the night when he was asleep at home, leaving him with no provable alibi.

The government claimed to have DNA evidence proving that Michael was present at the scene of these crimes. One of the crimes in question was the murder and subsequent burning

---

1   http://clclt.com/charlotte/the-tarnished-legacy-of-retiring-da-peter-gilchrist/
     Content?oid=2176238.
2   Ibid.

of Michael's mentor and his entire family. This man was like a father to Michael, who vigorously disputed that he was involved in the murder in any way.

Michael asked his attorney to get this DNA evidence that supposedly proved he was guilty of murder. Since he had been close to the victims and had been in and out of their home for years, his DNA was bound to be in the house. But that house, and all the DNA in it, had been burned after the murder(s). The government covered this problem by claiming that they had Michael's DNA from *inside* one of the burned victims—something Michael knew was not true. He knew whatever alleged DNA evidence they were using would prove his innocence, and hopefully indicate who had brutally murdered his surrogate family.

But Michael's attorney refused to have the DNA evidence analyzed or to challenge the prosecutor at trial. Whether he was just incompetent or deliberately sold Michael out to the prosecutor is still unclear, but what is clear is that Michael was sentenced to death. He is on death row based on false evidence and lies by a prosecutor who was angry that he had to go to trial—and he's not alone. North Carolina has been ordered to release several of its death-row inmates over the past four years due to similarly false prosecutions using phony, fabricated, and nonexistent evidence.[3]

During the months and years following his sentence, Michael pressed to challenge his death sentence. His requests were completely ignored—until we began writing about his case.

In 2012, Attorney Robert Trenckle took an interest in Michael's case and began investigating it—something that apparently had not been done before by either the government or Michael's own attorney(s). I worked with Trenckle

---

3 Mandy Locke, Joseph Neff, and J. Andrew Curliss, "Scathing SBI audit says 230 cases tainted by shoddy investigations," *The News & Observer*, August 19, 2010.

on the investigation, and we reviewed what we knew about Michael's very consistent claims of innocence and the alleged DNA evidence that would prove that government had lied at his trial. Trenckle filed motion after motion for this evidence in the North Carolina courts, until a judge finally ordered the government to turn over its alleged evidence.

But, the government could not comply. The DNA evidence the prosecutor claimed to have at Michael's trial many years before—had mysteriously *gone missing*.

Michael wrote, "But as slow as these people go, Woltz, I will probably die of old age before I get this straightened out. Took three years to get them to look at the DNA evidence again!" His letter went on to say, "But as you and I know, the truth doesn't have to set you free here anymore. But at least I got hope again!"

So Michael Sherrill received a death sentence for a North Carolina "cold case" based on just two factors: 1) the knowingly unreliable testimony of a jailhouse snitch who was compensated by a reduction in his own sentence and 2) the unproven claim to a jury by a public prosecutor of having DNA evidence which did not exist.

Still, why did the government take the case against Michael so far? The answer may lie in the fact that, at the time, the federal government was giving Mecklenburg County and other local governments millions of dollars for solving so-called "cold cases." In a conversation with a former Mecklenburg County prosecutor, I learned the reason for this could be traced to a TV show called *The Closer*,[4] which made the topic of solving cold cases popular with the public.

The federal government wanted to exploit this newfound interest in cold cases for publicity—and I suspect to repair

---

4 A TNT Original Series aired between 2005–2012 starring Kyra Sedgwick as Deputy Police Chief Brenda Johnson, who runs the Priority Homicide Division of the LAPD, solving "cold cases"; http://www.imdb.com/title/tt0458253/.

some of the lack of trust in public prosecutors' reputations, which were already quite sullied, even back then. Meanwhile, the Mecklenburg County D.A.'s office wanted the money the feds were offering, so they offered not to kill Michael Sherrill if he would just plead guilty to *any* murder. According to Michael's recollection, it didn't matter which murder he chose as long as it happened many years before. They even told him that in exchange for pleading guilty, they would release him immediately as "time served." My theory (and that of the prosecutor, who spoke confidentially about this situation) is that Mecklenburg County wanted to get and keep all the federal money without having to spend any of it on a trial.

I've worked with Michael's defense team for some time now, and in September of 2014, just days before his second trial on "cold case" charges was scheduled to begin, we were informed that the state agreed to drop all of the *seven* capital charges— all of which Michael has long claimed he could prove false with adequate investigation (and an attorney working for him rather than the prosecutor). An appeal on the charge for which he's already on death row is now being prepared, based on the fact that the "gone missing" evidence was claimed to the jury to be in hand at his trial to convict him. ("Gone missing," in my experience, translates to "we never had it.")

Despite his pending appeal and my 100 percent faith in his innocence, I fear that this man will still die for a crime committed in 1984 that the state cannot honestly claim or prove he committed—and that no one who knows Michael would believe him capable of doing. His case and others like it still haunt me, even a decade later. In fact, I received a letter from Michael Sherrill recently detailing the events of January 7, 2016. That day was Michael's 60th birthday, and his letter told me what it was like to celebrate it on death row.

Michael wrote that he is tiring of a battle that seemingly has no end. He expressed his personal anguish at what had been taken from him by the state of North Carolina and admitted to breaking down and crying over it all on his 60th birthday, quietly, in his cell. He grieved at having missed his mother's funeral and those of many of other friends and family members who have died during his lengthy incarceration. As he so poignantly wrote to me back in 2013, "But as you and I know, the truth doesn't have to set you free here anymore."

I believe that Michael Sherrill is a victim of kidnapping by the state of North Carolina. The judge and prosecutor—acting under color of law when they committed their crime(s)—have done a great harm to society. They not only illegally deprived a citizen of liberty, they lessened respect for the institutions they swore to uphold and reduced respect for the law.

As Supreme Court Justice Louis D. Brandeis once wrote, "If the government becomes the lawbreaker, it breeds contempt for law . . ."[5]

Having a system of justice peopled by judges, prosecutors, and agents who are themselves serial criminals according to our laws, but are somehow protected from penalty, renders our system to be one of "injustice" instead. It is time to return to the Constitutional requirement of equal treatment of all citizens under (and by) the law.

---

5 www.brainyquote.com/quotes/quotes/l/louisdbra105437.html.

CHAPTER 9

Establish an Office of Ombudsman

Albert Einstein is often quoted as saying that the definition of insanity is doing the same thing over and over again and expecting a different result. That is what is currently happening with America's judicial system, and one of the reasons behind our mass incarceration crisis. The same individuals, doing the same thing they have done for three decades, are unlikely to produce anything better or different than what we now have. It is even less likely that they will suddenly begin policing themselves, or charging one another with crimes committed against We the People.

Clearly, we cannot trust these same individuals to fix the problem they have created. Yet this is exactly what needs to happen before any real change can occur.

Of course, the United States is not the only nation in history ever to face this sort of crisis. Societies throughout history have found themselves in similar circumstances—and those who have successfully fought and overcome systemic corruption all have one thing in common: At some point in their history, they established an Office of Ombudsman.

According to my research, Sweden was the first country to establish an office where an elected official, independent of government itself, was given the authority to hear citizens' grievances against those in authority and then take independent action against individuals in government who violated the rights of the citizenry. Denmark, Finland, and Norway followed Sweden's lead and established their own Offices of

Ombudsman. The results have been impressive—in 2013, *The Economist* described these four countries as "probably the best-governed in the world."[1]

Research has shown that, time and time again, nations with corrupt and scandal-ridden governments have been transformed once an independent elected party is given the power and authority to do something about it. In fact, of the 140 nations that claim to be free and democratic, 139 of them have followed Sweden's example and have Ombudsman Offices in each district. The one holdout out of those 140 free and democratic nations? The United States of America.

Our leaders are the only ones in the democratic world who have refused to give power to an independent authority with the duty and wherewithal to make them follow the law. Is it any wonder we have more citizens wrongfully convicted and imprisoned than any country in the world, when we are the only one without having any means to bring criminals of government to justice themselves?

It is time to force our leaders to join the rest of the civilized world and establish Offices of Ombudsman in every federal district in the United States of America. If government can afford an Office of U.S. Attorney to attack citizens in every district, it can afford an Office of Ombudsmen to keep them honest.

The Constitution provides for establishment of these independent courts in Section 1 of Article III: "The judicial power of the United States, shall be vested in one Supreme Court, and in such inferior courts as the Congress may from time to time ordain and establish. The judges, both of the supreme and inferior courts, shall hold their offices during good behaviour, and shall, at stated times, receive for their services, a compensation, which shall not be diminished during their continuance in office."

---

1 "The Secret of Their Success," The Economist, February 2, 2013.

To ensure their independence and impartiality, these offices should not be appointed or political in any way. Section 1 of Article III does not specify any particular method of choosing, which frees Congress to establish 94 such offices, to be filled through non-partisan elections, the only stated requirement of office being that the chief ombudsman reside in the congressional district where he or she presides.

This single act has the power to put an end to the suffering of knowingly innocent prisoners left to languish in jail for decades, and to give the wrongfully convicted a prompt and efficient means of being heard by someone other than those who committed the crimes against them. The ombudsman will be able to take action against prosecutors found to have knowingly convicted the innocent, as well as any government agent, judge or employee who knowingly violated the rights of the citizen under color of law. These statutes already exist—the ombudsman only needs to enforce them. Congress should also add the crimes of knowingly prosecuting the innocent and violating constitutional rights under color of law to the short list of heinous offenses like murder and rape which have no statute of limitations, as many of the victims of this crime are languishing in prison years after those who wrongfully put them there are eligible for punishment. After the first few judges and prosecutors are sentenced to federal prison, fined, and forced to pay restitution to their victims, mass incarceration will cease to be a problem, and Rule of Law will again have meaning in our land.

Should our Congress continue to refuse to take meaningful action, the states can take the lead by establishing Offices of Ombudsman themselves, and craft legislation that places all officials—state or federal—under the authority of the ombudsman to prosecute the violation of citizens' rights under state law. Federal courts have ruled that, "State courts do retain the power to afford their residents greater protection for certain liberties established by their own state constitution than is afforded by the federal Constitution,"[2] so a state-established Office of Ombudsmen, giving greater protection to the citizen, would take constitutional precedence over the current federal system, where justice is precluded. Once one or two states establish Offices of Ombudsmen and send federal judges and prosecutors to prison for their crimes, Congress is more likely to wake up and act, if only to regain some level of federal control over the process.

ACTION ITEMS FOR ESTABLISHING AN OFFICE OF OMBUDSMAN

1. Under Article III of the United States Constitution, Congress should establish Offices of Ombudsman as elected positions in each federal district in the United States, with the independent authority 1) to grant relief to citizens whose rights are violated by government and 2) to independently prosecute anyone who violates a citizens' rights under color of law.

2. Absent congressional action to establish a national system of Ombudsmen Offices, states should legislatively establish such courts and vest them with the authority to investigate and prosecute any government officials—including federal ones—who violate the rights of their citizens within the state's borders—and vest them with the power to grant immediate relief to the victims.[3]

---

2 Prune Yard Shopping Center v. Robins, 447 U.S. 74, 100 S. Ct. 2035, 64 L. Ed. 2d 741 [1980].

3 The conviction of federal judges, agents, and prosecutors who violate law by state ombudsmen would inevitably be challenged by the federal Department of Justice, as would court orders issued by state ombudsmen for relief (and release) in cases of wrongful conviction of their citizens or in federal courts located within their borders, but the stage would then be set for a challenge of the unconstitutionality of placing these individuals above the

What Is an Ombudsman?

No Office of Ombudsman has yet been established in the United States to right the wrongs of government gone astray, so there is no "story" to tell for this chapter. However, it may be worthwhile to provide more information as to what this office *could* do to solve the incarceration crisis and heal our nation.

According to Wikipedia, "An ombudsman or public advocate is usually appointed by the government or by parliament, but with a significant degree of independence, who is charged with representing the interests of the public by investigating and addressing complaints of maladministration or a violation of rights."[1]

Who could possibly be against such a thing? The answer appears to be "everyone in state or federal government in the USA today," according to those *in* government whom I have asked to support this idea. Perhaps because the current structure of America's justice system would shatter under independent inspection by an elected office with the power to prosecute judges and prosecutors who have committed "violation[s] of rights" during the performance of their public duties.

However, the judicial branch of our government is hardly the only branch that could not survive this sort of scrutiny. Every week, the legislative branch passes laws that are so far

law—or forcing Congress to address the problems it has created and/or allowed.

1 https://en.wikipedia.org/wiki/Ombudsman.

beyond that body's allocated authority that they could be considered criminal acts of usurpation of power. The punishment of 314,000 human behaviors which are constitutionally outside of the legal purview granted Congress by the Constitution is but one example. The delegation of that body's lawmaking authority to unelected agencies is another. Not long ago, such acts would have been considered treason, and those who committed them would be tried and hung for their crimes.

Meanwhile, since World War II, the Executive Branch has unilaterally started over 180 wars and military actions without the Congressional approval required by the Constitution. Each of these actions were grounds for that president's impeachment. Presidents also now routinely legislate from the White House using the power of "Executive Order"—a power found nowhere in the Constitution—and have used it to unilaterally create a host of spy agencies including the FBI, CIA, NSA (and sixteen others) that continue to endanger, rather than protect, our liberties, privacy, and national security.

Rather than enforce the Constitution and put a stop to this federal lawlessness, the Supreme Court has been asleep at the wheel. Instead, this third branch of government has indicated that it, too, is up for sale, as evidenced by the string of cases beginning in 1886, and culminating in the *Citizens United* decision we explored earlier, which basically handed the keys to our country to the multinational corporations who can now buy, sell (and rent) our elected representatives.

It is clear why none of these entities want to establish a truly independent office with the powers to investigate and prosecute them. They are all acting outside of law and authority granted them by the United States Constitution. That is also why we need this office more than ever.

Perhaps because of the poor example the United States has set by failing to abide by its founding principles, when the European Union was established, leadership in Brussels included an Office of Ombudsman to hold themselves accountable to their citizenry. The office has a website any EU member nation, citizen, or resident can access, which states, "If you are a citizen of a Member State of the Union or reside in a Member State, you can make a complaint to the European Ombudsman. Businesses, associations or other bodies with a registered office in the Union may also complain to the Ombudsman."

An independent law enforcement office that represents We the People instead of the government should not be feared by anyone—with the exception of those who are acting in violation of our nation's laws. Establishing an Office of Ombudsman is an idea whose time has not only come, but is way overdue, and should become a litmus test for political candidates we support.

CHAPTER 10

Put Limits on Power

At both the federal and state level, the United States Constitution strictly limited the authority of those in power to prosecute and punish the citizenry they served. States, which were tasked with making and enforcing all laws regarding conduct other than piracy, counterfeiting and treason, were also required to follow the severe restraints established by the Bill of Rights. Everyone who governs in America still swears to abide by these documents when taking their oath of office. However, authorities at both levels of government have basically shackled these rights or routinely ignore them without consequence.

Prosecutions are now usurped from states by federal authorities, outside of their constitutional purview. This is especially common in drug cases—agencies such as the Drug Enforcement Agency have infiltrated local sheriff departments and police forces to the point that they are more like appendages of Washington than autonomously operated entities of a separate sovereign government. This further erodes the checks and balances between state and federal authority as they are—constitutionally—two separate sovereignties, on equal footing. One is not superior, as their powers were intended to be divided, with the state actually being the more powerful.

The influence of federal power and its questionable methods on state and local law enforcement has been a negative one. The worst fears expressed by the anti-federalists in their arguments against a strong(er) federal government during the 1780s have all been far exceeded by reality.

On April 18, 2015, Spencer S. Hsu's *Washington Post* column opened with the following sentence: "The Justice Department and FBI have formally acknowledged that nearly every examiner in an elite FBI forensic unit gave flawed testimony in almost all trials in which they offered evidence against criminal defendants over more than a two-decade period before 2000."

This single sentence defines the problem that has caused mass incarceration in America. Our Executive Branch's two "justice" authorities have admitted to lying and falsifying evidence at criminal trials—for decades.

If the FBI (which runs criminal investigations all over the world) and the Department of Justice (which does the prosecuting) have jointly admitted that they "gave flawed testimony *in almost all trials in which they offered evidence* against criminal defendants *over more than a two-decade period . . .*" clearly our federal government needs to get out of the criminal prosecution business.

How did these constitutionally unauthorized agencies come to operate as "Executive Branch" police forces in the first place? Where is that in the Constitution?[1] These bad actors have tainted our system of justice to the point that recovery is unlikely, as the rot has already spread from the federal level to the states.

In 2010, *News & Observer* reporters Mandy Locke and Joseph Neff did a series on the serial corruption in the State Bureau of

---

[1] Neither the FBI or Department of Justice are constitutional federal entities, as there is no constitutional provision for a federal police force, nor an executive-controlled means of controlling all prosecutions. The FBI was, in fact, rejected by the U.S. Congress as unconstitutional when it was proposed by President Theodore Roosevelt in 1907 as an unrecognized power of federal government, and the Department of Justice was unlawfully created by the Republican Congress and President Ulysses S. Grant while the Southern states were not part of the Union, and never lawfully passed, if the argument for their invasion was that they could not leave the union. The creation of new executive powers—unrecognized or authorized by the U.S. Constitution, would have required their approval as well.

Investigation—an agency that was trained and reviewed by FBI forensic experts. Locke and Neff discovered that evidence in the state agency had been falsified, withheld, faked, and created, and juries had been misled—also for decades. It is rather obvious where they learned the tricks of their illicit trade.

How did we wind up with the FBI, which is essentially a national police force, in the first place? President Theodore Roosevelt initially approached Congress about creating it, but was refused. Congress cited as its reason the fact that such as national police force was (and still is) unconstitutional. Senator Benjamin "Pitchfork" Tillman of South Carolina gave this opinion on behalf of Congress—and was subsequently banned from visiting the White House by the president.

Undaunted, President Roosevelt created his Federal Bureau of Investigation using the tool we now know as Executive Order. No such power can be found in Article II of the U.S. Constitution, yet presidents frequently (and illegally) legislate from the Executive Branch using this method without challenge, almost every week,[2] often creating more legislation than the body which has that exclusive power—the U.S. Congress. Roosevelt's Attorney General, Charles Bonaparte (Emperor Napoleon Bonaparte's grand-nephew) was put in charge of this national police force. Within days, his men were caught breaking in to Senator Tillman's office in Congress and going through the Senator's mail.

Today as then, the FBI acts under and reports directly to the nation's chief politician, the president, and is an Executive Branch department. It has never been legally authorized, and is nowhere to be found in the Constitution as a power or proper entity of the federal government.

---

2 It may be of interest to the reader to know that the first unlawful "Executive Order" was issued when President Abraham Lincoln illegally suspended *habeas corpus* in 1861, as discussed in Chapter 1.

The United States Department of Justice has an equally inauspicious and little known beginning, as it is not authorized by the Constitution either. Established in 1870 by President Ulysses S. Grant and his Republican Congress before the Southern states rejoined the Union (to avoid their strenuous objections), this agency was created to give the president authority over federal prosecutions, likely for political purposes. That is still its function today, as recently evidenced by the Obama Administration's attacks on conservative groups at a ratio of approximately 7:1, Republicans to Democrats. Obama's predecessor, Republican President George W. Bush, prosecuted Democrats at the same rate and ratio—7:1, Democrats to Republicans. In other words, neither party holds the franchise on this abuse of power.

Born outside of the Union's wedlock as a tool of executive abuse, the DOJ remains one today as evidenced by both 1) the statistics (a 7:1 incrimination of opponents) and 2) the admitted criminal conduct of the FBI and Department of Justice in "almost every" prosecutions over decades. Like the FBI, the DOJ is an Executive Branch department, acting under and reporting directly to the head of whichever political party is in power. He (or she) then appoints the prosecutors in all 94 federal districts and offices, and the game of "get the other side" begins once more in earnest. And, as Spencer S. Hsu reported, both of these Executive Branch agencies have now admitted to a criminal conspiracy to deprive thousands of U.S. citizens of their right of due process over decades. Together, these two executive departments have put thousands of innocents behind bars, and in some cases, to death. Their tactics have been present to some degree in all of the 400 plus criminal cases I have worked on between 2006 and 2013.

The Columbia Law School study discussed in the first chapter showed that the courts erred in 73 percent of death penalty (capital) cases. My own research of hundreds of noncapital cases revealed DOJ attorneys and these executive agencies broke the law in every single case where I assisted in filing motions. That is a 100 percent error rate, not just 73 percent as the courts themselves admitted.

There is no *fix* or reform for these agencies. They simply need to go away. I have yet to read of either the FBI or the Department of Justice allocating any resources to righting these intentional wrongs—wrongs that were only acknowledged when independent groups and law schools uncovered them. These injustices were (and are) *intentionally* committed, yet no court or government agency is willing to offer the government's victims relief. This is a sad day for our nation.

In 2013, I quit working on these cases. It was simply too heartbreaking to see the same criminal conduct by our government and courts over and over again and know that there was no hope of correcting it. So I began writing about the corruption I witnessed, hoping to expose these injustices to a wider audience.

I have spent 10 years now working on individual cases of injustice, and I'm still waiting for those who committed these injustices to release their victims. It is high time to put the genie back in the bottle. We need to put the federal government, its appendages, its "quasi-federal" lawmakers, its political operatives acting as agents and prosecutors—all of them—on notice that We the People have reached the breaking point. This is our country, and we have a contract with federal government of which they are now in breach.

That contract is the United States Constitution, and every one of these bad actors, who swore to uphold it, is trashing it instead. There are 312 million of *us* at last count, and only 545 of *them*—435 in the House of Representatives, 100 in the Senate, nine serving as Supreme Court Justices, and one president. These 545 people caused these problems, and are also the only people who presently have the power to solve them and return our nation to Rule of Law.

In all but a few rare cases, our current batch of representatives, senators, Supreme Court justices, and our nation's chief politician have demonstrated that they lack the political will to do something about our current crisis. Yes, they are all talking about it now—but only because so many of *us* are talking about it, on both sides of the political divide. Real action, however, remains all but absent, as all 545 of these individuals have a large stake in keeping the *status quo*. The reality is, most of those now in power thrive on the current state of affairs, and many are deeply invested in the prison industry via donations, dividends, or threat of defeat in the next election if they attempt to address the scandal of mass incarceration.

Dismantling the FBI and Department of Justice may be the right and constitutional thing to do. Few Americans are aware that both of these departments were conceived in sin, outside of the law and the Constitution, or that we ever survived (and did far better) as a nation without them. However, the nation has become so accustomed to these organizations being in power that it sounds foreign—almost insane—to talk about putting them back in the unconstitutional hole from which they sprang.

One day these ideas will not sound so foreign. If we can restore our Constitution and force government officials to uphold it rather than tearing it down, questions about such unconstitutional entities will be raised as a matter of course. The existence of such unconstitutional agencies and powers will one day be challenged. But at this point, the time may not yet be right to eliminate them once and for all.

So instead of recommending the dismantling of these agencies as an action item, I am making another suggestion. I propose only that we go back to the constitutional method of supporting candidates for office. This method worked quite well, and our nation did not go too far astray, until we abandoned it.

Prior to 1886, if a corporation or nonhuman entity outside of his district of election gave a politician money, it was considered what it was—a bribe. Then came the case known as *Santa Clara County v. Southern Pacific Railroad,* which changed the political landscape and created the corporate-controlled Congress and White House that we have today. *Santa Clara* was little more than an innocuous, uninteresting tax case, known for neither its facts nor its holding on the issue. What makes the case significant is a single offhand remark from Justice Morrison Remick Waite, which was made from the bench before the beginning of oral arguments even began. He said, "The court does not wish to hear argument on the question whether the provision in the Fourteenth Amendment to the Constitution, which forbids a State to deny to any person within its jurisdiction the equal protection of the laws, applies to these corporations. We are all of opinion that it does."

This offhand two-sentence comment by a single Justice elevated corporations to the status of people under the law (in the opinion of J.P. Morgan's corporate attorneys) and created the doctrine of legal personhood.[3] As we already discussed in Chapter 8, there is no mention of corporations in the Constitution—not because they did not exist, but because the Constitution did not apply to them. They were not and are not "We the People" the party of the first part to our contract with our Government.

It is clear we need a complete change of leadership in this nation before these problems will be resolved. None of the present players in any of the three branches of our federal government are the answer, and both political parties have been bought off by the same corporate donors.[4] They have collectively given us the system of mass incarceration and corporate control of our nation under which we all suffer today. But this nation is ours, and we need to take it back before it is too late.

Action Item 10 provides a way to do this with just one law or constitutional amendment. We need to return to what worked, and limit any donation to any politician to those living, breathing

---

3 *Santa Clara v. Southern Pacific Railroad* 118 U.S. 394 (1886).
4 The Forbes 500.

human beings who reside in their district of election. No one else. No corporations. No people from other districts. No foreign citizens or their governments. No PACS. Not even political parties have the right to buy my Representative, and they should be restricted from doing so under criminal penalty of law.

If James Madison had written our contract between government on the one hand, and We the People, the corporations, PACs, unions, and political parties on the other, I could not make this argument. But that is not what our founders wrote, contemplated, or would ever have agreed to let happen. This contract, our Constitution was between We the *People* and our government. No one else was a party to the contract, and those other entities only give money expecting something in return.[5] We must limit the donation of any money, gift, service, or assistance to politicians running for office to those who live and reside in their districts of election, and politics will quickly return to a job of service rather than a way to get rich from political donations. America will slowly right itself. Rule of Law will reappear.

When the prison industry can no longer buy our politicians, the gross injustice of it all will become horrifying to those who once looked the other way while taking prison blood money as political donations to create the system. In fact, if billions of dollars were not changing hands to buy our politicians for corporate and other interests, that alone would allow our nation to move past this crisis point. The military would once again revert to defending us, rather than bankrupting us as a mercenary force for corporate interests. No banks would be "too big to fail," and no citizens who run them would be above the law when they break it. Lobbyists would have to get real jobs, as our representatives would no longer be for sale to the highest

---

5 "Multiple studies have shown that corporate spending, particularly on lobbying, yields returns of as much as 6 times the money spent in terms of tax breaks and other benefits" quoted in "Why Don't Investors Get to Opt Out of Corporate Political Contributions?" by Daniel Fisher, *Forbes* magazine.

corporate bidder, union, political party, foreign government, or professional monopoly. Our representatives' concern would return to Main Street back home, as opposed to K Street in the District of Columbia.

One change—that's all—and we can save our nation.

ACTION ITEM FOR PUTTING LIMITS ON POWER

1. Pass just one law—that only living, breathing citizens residing in the district wherein an election shall be held, can donate cash or kind to the campaign or person running for any public office.

Let's take our country back.

INDEX

Howell W. Woltz, TEP, was a trust and estate practitioner by profession until 2006. He has also been a public speaker, journalist and writer on the issues of freedom and the erosion of rights guaranteed by the United States Constitution for almost 40 years.

Born in Mt. Airy, North Carolina, Woltz attended the University of Virginia, where he studied economics, with graduate studies at Wake Forest MBA School and Caledonian University in Glasgow, Scotland. He delivered his first speech about American rights and rule of law in 1977, warning that the United States was on the road to becoming like the (now) former Soviet Union. He has since seen many of his original predictions come true.

In an ironic twist, Woltz now lives and writes in the former Soviet Bloc, in Warsaw, Poland, with his wife, Dr. Magdalena Iwaniec-Woltz. He is also studying at the University of Warsaw's Polonicum, while continuing to speak and write about the importance of rule of law in human society.

NOTE TO READER

I began researching and writing this book in 2015, when I was still living in the United States. It was a project that would, I have since concluded, ultimately force me to leave my country less than a year later.

The previous year, I delivered a TED talk on the need for judicial reform in the United States.[1] That speech led to many other speaking engagements and TV presentations on the subject, proving my message was resonating with the public. I decided to take it a step further by writing a book offering concrete solutions to our mass incarceration crisis.

Soon after the TED talk, I started receiving death threats—almost always when I was preparing for another presentation on the subject of justice reform. These calls were always routed from abroad, always came in the middle of the night, and were spaced over a period of several weeks. When I researched the telephone numbers the calls originated from, I learned they did not exist, something I have since been told is a standard tactic employed to silence whistleblowers and journalists who report about issues that might sully the U.S. government's image.

In case that wasn't enough to make their point, I also received several menacing visits from U.S. federal agents, warning me to quit speaking out about the erosion of freedom in America and threatening me with "problems" if I did not "shut-up."

I did not "shut up"—and that's when the real terror campaign began. Now, family members and friends were being threatened and warned that I should stop speaking and writing,

1 https://www.youtube.com/watch?v=BPvfi-Je97o.

or they would become targets of IRS audits and prosecution for unidentified crimes. I was personally threatened by U.S. marshals on two occasions, on behalf of a corrupt North Carolina judge about whom I had written. Then came break-ins by gun-wielding federal agents, along with threats of prosecution against my family and friends who had assisted me in places from Raleigh, where that judge still presides, to Roanoke, Virginia, and New York City.

I wound up selling or giving away everything I had. I was literally living out of my car, going from family member to friend trying to finish a new book, *Gulag Amerika,* between speeches and threats. I was also becoming more and more aware that I was endangering the same friends and family who were taking me in.

Then one day, my car was broken into in broad daylight, in a U.S. Post Office parking lot. The thieves took only my briefcase, left a key scratch down the passenger side of the car, and locked it again, to make it clear that my electronic key—which had been stolen from a friend's house where I had been staying four months before—had been used. I had been using my spare key ever since, wondering when something like this would happen . . . and where.

Within an hour of the theft, I received a call on my cell phone with a warning that the briefcase (with my laptop, digital copies of my writings, money, passport, etc.), would be left in the home of the feds' next "target." When I returned to my brother's house in Roanoke, VA, where I was staying, my briefcase was inside the front door. Everything was in it. Not a paper clip was missing.

I realized it was time to leave the "Land of the Free" and the home I loved.

Without telling anyone where I was going, I took a bus from Roanoke, Virginia, to the nearest Amtrak station and took the train to New York City. I met with my literary agent, as well as a wonderful director who had the courage to do an award-winning film on my story,[2] to thank them for their courage and to say goodbye.

Then I caught a direct flight to Warsaw, Poland. I have not been back to the United States of America since.

I believe my story serves as an example and a warning of what can and will happen to more and more citizens if we don't take action and take our country back. We've become that which we once fought against—or as I remember from an old Pogo cartoon years ago:

"I have seen the enemy and it is us."

---

2 https://vimeo.com/67788075.

CPSIA information can be obtained
at www.ICGtesting.com
Printed in the USA
LVOW04s0532251016
510159LV00014B/464/P